Transformational Acting

Transformational Acting

A Step Beyond

Sande Shurin

Limelight Editions • New York

First Limelight Edition, November 2002

Interior design by Rachel Reiss

Manufactured in the United States of America

Library of Congress Cataloging-in-Publication data will be furnished by the publisher upon request.

Dedication

To my husband Bruce Levy, the unsung hero of this book. For his brilliant contributions and insistence on clarity, his commitment to a magnificent life together, and for turning our dreams into reality.

To my daughter Stephanie Kaplan, whose teenage years led me to prayer and whose love I cherish.

Heartfelt Thanks...

To my students and teachers of "The Shurin Technique," Transformational Acting, who share my love of brilliance, creativity, and transformation. To: my friend Tripp Hanson, Ginger Prince, Anthony Rapp, Christianne Tisdale, Suzan Perry, Anitra Frazier, Jadah Carroll, Jenni Frost, Hope Jackson, Scott Darby, Mark Kassen, Ben Golden, Dr. Alan Pressman; Bill Kalatsky, Lainy Reicher, and my agent Lewis Chambers... Paul Savas for his sensitive and astute editing

And to: Mel Zerman... thank you again and again for your vision, integrity, and contribution to this book.

Gratitude...

God, my teachers and guides: Baba Muktananda, Werner Erhard, Marianne Williamson and to My Higher Self

To my mother Mildred, and my two dads Martin and Robert

To Aunt Rita Fromm and my late Uncle Martin Fromm, my mother-in-law Mildred Levy, Judy and Jeff Fisher, Mitch and Ellie Morse, and my brothers Isak Linndenaeur and Aaron Shurin.

God Bless!

Preface

I've been acting since I was six years old (professionally since I was nine), and I've encountered a number of mentors and teachers and directors over the years who have made an impact on my life and my work. But none of them has had the kind of staying power of influence and inspiration as Sande Shurin has had with me, for over twelve years now.

I have long desired to see her name rise to the level of recognition of the other great and respected acting teachers of the past—Stanislavsky, Lee Strasberg, Stella Adler, Sanford Meisner, to name a few. I see no reason on earth why this shouldn't be possible for Sande, and my sincere hope is that with the publication of this book it will be a *fait accompli*.

The work she had done with me over the years, and the work I have witnessed her bring out in so many other actors, has such breadth and depth and scope, and is applicable to any kind of role or venue or medium. I have done a fair amount of teaching myself in the past several years, giving master classes based in Sande's technique at such schools as Ithaca College, Utah State University, Syracuse University, and Interlochen Arts Academy, among many others, and I have found that her technique, which I have honed over the years through working with Sande, has resonated with all of the students at all of those schools; all of which have foundations in many different approaches to the work of creating a character, of becoming an actor. Again and again, the feedback I get from the instructors at those schools is that my teaching only reinforces and builds on the work they had been doing with their students all along. I can only say that this acknowledges even more deeply the efficacy and power of Sande's technique.

Being an actor is a great privilege: to be able to see and experience the world through other people's eyes—fictional characters' eyes—and therefore open up our audiences to new horizons, new ways of thinking, new vistas of understanding. I have always loved acting, but through my work with Sande my relationship to my art and craft has only deepened, become more pure, and I will never be able to express enough gratitude to her.

I hope you find a little bit of that magic as you read this book.

—*Anthony Rapp*
July, 2002

Foreword

I love brilliance!
... including *great* actors, *great* techniques and *great* acting teachers. There's room and purpose for all... a variety of techniques for different personalities.

Sense memory brings actors back to their own personal histories. Through their senses, they can use their life-experiences... and their wounds... with the accompanying emotions, to work into the role. If deep psychological exploration is your bent, this might be a good place to explore.

As for Sanford Meisner, there are some fine teachers, putting their actors through repetition and preparation exercises, utilizing imagination and calling you into the future with the acting standard "if" ... a methodical technique where spontaneity is the desired result.

For me, I want to see my actors fly. I want to see them soar beyond their thoughts into the unknown... bold always risking and with "edge." Transformational Acting is the structure that gets you there while providing you with an electric performance, daring actions, compelling behavior and your own constantly changing voice cutting together with the character's voice—a deep exploration and melding of the "self" and "character."

Those actors drawn to my technique have a propensity for higher awareness and self-exploration, including actors already trained in Method and Meisner, who want more of their current selves infused in the work.

Through my technique the actors find themselves more presenced, infused in the work and aware.

God bless all of us!

With this book actors take a step-by-step journey into knowing themselves; they use "self" as the raw material to transform into character.

For creating, we tap into an active energy and intelligence alive in all of nature. This unifying intelligence and dynamic energy already exists inside each and every one of us. This essence is the source of my new approach.

In Transformational Acting, the actor is taught to access this essence along with the "Emotional Body" (a new way to generate current emotions without having to rely on histrionics). Strong new acting distinctions are also taught in this technique, such as transforming who *You* are into *That* character—actually reinventing yourself as the character. It's about you, who you are, what you bring to the character, and using what is relevant from within you. This new acting technique takes the actor beyond "Sense Memory" into Transformational Acting.

Life occurs. The bell rings. The baby cries. The food burns. We don't sit and wait for "it" to happen. When "it" occurs we grunt, mutter, moan, make noises, say words...we respond... but first comes life, then the words become illuminated.

To work in this truth is to create the life without predetermining. This includes the actions, relationships, dynamics and emotions beneath and before the words. It takes true listening and responding. It takes being in the moments and open to new and sometimes extraordinary possibilities that being in touch with your "universal truth" provides.

The actor must be daring and risky; he must defy habits, boundaries, limitations and conventions. It takes living and acting from the silent space within ourselves; this inner creative mode affords you the brilliance and freedom to transform into what you've not yet become. It yields an enlivening experience for actor, audience and even as a lifestyle for any and all human beings.

I began to develop this new acting technique in 1980; or rather it began to create itself through me—and continues to do so. It surprises me everyday as I hope it will you.

Contents

PART ONE

An Overview of Transformational Acting

CHAPTER 1

The Evolution of Transformational Acting

The Formative Years

I began in the 1960s. Not my physical birth—my artistic birth. Everything that is said about the 1960s is true—it was an exciting and provocative time. The spirit of change ran high. At Berkeley protests against the war in Vietnam began, and universally women were liberated by birth control pills. It was a time of political upheaval and cultural change. People found their own voices as draft cards were burned, bras came off and sexuality became an everyday sport.

Now, at about that time I wanted to be an actress and realized that, unlike the legendary Lana Turner, I was not going to be discovered at Schwab's drugstore. Instead I would have to take action to get things to work out. So, on the strength of a simple, stark, eye-catching ad in the *Village Voice*. I enrolled at Irene Dailey's School of the Actor's Company in Greenwich Village to study acting.

In her own inimitable style, Irene taught traditional Stanislavsky method infused with concepts she had learned in her studies with Uta Hagen and Tony Manino. The curriculum she developed included object exploration, sense memory, the fourth wall and animal exercises. Irene had quite a notable name at the time, having starred on Broadway in *The Subject was Roses.*

What inspired me most were Irene's precept that "every situation is special and particular" along with her focus on the character's life before the time frame presented in the play. These ideas intrigued me. Irene would guide actors through an improvisation exercise on a period of time in the character's life not occurring within the play. What the actors had discovered about the character in this exercise they would bring into the actual moments of the play. It was a revelation for me to consider that a character has a life other than what the audience sees.

By 1966, I was traveling to Manhattan, studying acting and hanging out at the old Limelight Cafe, Pennyfeather's Restaurant on Seventh Avenue South, and Jane Street's Corner Bistro, talking with James Baldwin, Sudie Bond and other Greenwich Village regulars.

I was an actress, wife, and mother. Yet, I was restless and challenging my biggest fear—myself. TRANSCENDENCE became my life theme. I wanted to be lifted beyond everyday circumstances and ordinary reality. That's why Irene's classes meant so much to me. The new vistas she opened thrust me into a new stage in my life. Acting put everything in place for me. It left me with a feeling of possibility, with the first positive experience that helped me to transcend the pressures and responsibilities of my daily life. Healthful transcendence put me more in touch with myself. Working on plays organized my chaos. Acting was my doorway to clarity.

Early in my studies with Irene, she asked me to teach one of her classes while she rehearsed for the play *Rooms.* Among the students in my first class were two upcoming stars, David Soul and Kathleen Quinlan. This was not the first time I faced stepping into shoes that were much too big, but I walked straight into this opportunity and took another major turn in my life. My fierce desire for movement, as well as my not so easy temperament, helped me to redefine everything I had been taught, which led me to creating in a new way.

I began working with a group of actors, experimenting with new forms of theater. This group became my own ensemble acting company, Drifting Traffic. We rehearsed at night in a loft in the clock tower on Leonard Street in Lower Manhattan, which was provided by a grant from the New York Council on the Arts and shared with the Mabu Mines Theater Company.

To give the actors a chance to perform, our first venture, *"...and last week it was a mountain"* was a piece that I developed using movement, relationship, theme and concept as its spine. I also incorporated slides, paintings, video, music and movement. We had a very theatrical and visual experience but no script, so to weave the visual story together I had the actors perform the words of contemporary poets. Through this experience I learned the importance of the life and the dynamics under the words, and began to see the power of working from the silent space within—the emotions, the images, the experience and the feelings—rather than relying on words. This led me to artistic discoveries which fused self and character.

"Every line is an opportunity for a
physical/visual experience."

Drifting Traffic was one of the five groups that started the Off-Off Broadway Alliance (OOBA). The other groups were Jean Cocteau Theater, Playwrights Horizons, Will Lieberson's Blue

Dome, and La Mama. By banding together, we had an organization to "legitimize" us. With OOBA as the umbrella company, we all became members of the Cultural Council Foundation, which made us eligible for grants, bookkeeping services, seminars and hospitality services when we traveled overseas; it also entitled us to TDF's (Theater Development Fund) ticket vouchers to generate additional income, technical assistance programs, touring productions and festivals. The Cultural Council Foundation also provided attorneys through Volunteer Lawyers for the Arts.

It was an exhilarating time in the world of underground theater. The advent of OOBA sanctioned the unleashing of pure wild creativity in the form of innovative new plays and theater pieces; it also gave theater owners and producers the license to produce these spectacles to sometimes cheering, sometimes baffled, and yet amazed audiences.

We were all looking for a different kind of theater and when you are looking for a different kind of theater, you experiment. We experimented with exercises rather than working with plays. We worked with space: How can you move through space? What does my body feel like when I move through space? What does that take me to? What does the space make me want to do? We experimented vocally: What can we do with our voices? What can we do with silence? How can we express vocally? I guess this can be better understood through the technique now called Viewpoints. That is, exploring space, tempo, rhythms, dream movement, slow motion, speed, spatial relationship to the other actors. We investigated the shapes the body makes when taking full-range actions. I worked with the kind of groupings that formed from experiencing spatial relationships, and put some of them right into a play. It made us aware of our kinesthetic sense. Other exploration involved repetition, a full awareness of our responses to line, form, color, structure, shapes and the other actors.

My purpose in using exercises included developing openness, creativity, imagination, natural responses and physical visual pictures that expressed what was going on. This differed from the philosophical interplay with structure and other purposes that Viewpoints is constructed upon. We, in fact, created our own material through the use of these exercises. I loved that work.

The exercises themselves fascinated me. But I took them in a new direction: I presented these new theater forms within a traditional theatrical structure, bringing my experimental ability and passion to directing scripted plays.

> *"Follow the life, not the words,*
> *and the words will fall into place."*

In each directing project, I searched the material for the underlying dynamics and metaphors and for new visual forms with which to express and augment the drama. I went beyond the playwright's written words, using full scores of music in all of the plays I directed, a first at that time.

Transcendence, my favorite theme, ran through all of the work. I aimed to create experiences to take the audience beyond their everyday thoughts, notions and feelings, alter their points of view and shift their perceptions so they would go beyond their own walls and limitations and "stuck" points. "Blow their minds," the slogan of the day's prevailing consciousness groups, was also my anthem. To help me accomplish this I directed scripts that delved into extraordinary realities; or presented ordinary realities directed in a heightened, stylized and physical visual way.

My work, I am proud to say, was presented among that of Joe Chaikan, Sam Shepard, Maria Irene Fornes, Megan Terry, John Viccarro, Harvey Fierstein, Charles Ludlam, Tom O'Horgan, Crystal Field, George Bartienoff, Julie Bovasso and La Mama's Ellen Stewart.

"You have already chosen it; do it 100 percent."

By 1980, my new husband Bruce Levy and I had moved to a loft on West 17th Street in Chelsea. The actors who I had directed and coached were requesting steady classes. They all claimed to have had a qualitative shift in their acting work and life during our work together and wanted it to continue. Bruce suggested we open our own acting studio. Finally, I agreed to teach if I could develop a new system. After all I had been through, I couldn't go back to the old one.

It seemed to me that we needed a totally new context for acting and that a new technique would emerge from this context. I was different, people were different, and the whole culture was different from when I first taught method acting, which relied on past emotional experience. The technique I had taught merged with the popularity of psychotherapy. Emotions were still repressed and wounds were uncovered and utilized.

Transformational Acting came into being during the time of self-experience, self-realization and actualization. People were not holding onto the old ways but stepping into new possibilities. I wanted actors to have the immediacy and indefinable source of energy that many performers had. At the time I found it more exciting being at a Rolling Stones concert or watching David Bowie or Isaac Stern than sitting in a theater or at a film watching what might be an interesting concept but with no apparent transmission of life energy.

Through my directing and the fervor of the decade, I began to search for a new context, a new approach to teaching actors. I felt it was important for actors actually to go through an *experience* each time they performed. I wanted to create a new technique—one that would help actors grow continually and reach their potential, and when they reached that potential, create more potential. As part of this new context, I believed that actors needed to access and use currently occurring emotions and to do so in harmony with their own temperaments, rather than using a technique that requires recircuiting old memories.

> *"Live in a new clearing, not in your 'stuff' that has just been cleared."*

My goal was to create a technique that fostered acting as a moment-to-moment exhilarating challenge. Drawing on my experience from years of directing, I aimed to teach actors to tap into the raw, emotional energy of their selves so they could achieve greater depth and more aliveness in their performances.

In answer to a question I am asked most often, "Yes!" Transformational Acting works for all mediums."

> *"Acting is a conversation with a point of view."*

The inner work for all mediums is the same; only the expression is different. You need a creative technique first. That is your baseline. Then you can learn the specifics for theater, television and film. The trajectory is you. Because you are present and available and going through an experience, for a theater audience you will be palpable and for the camera you will open deeply. The way in which you respond for theater must be more prominent. Whereas for the subtleties and nuances in close-up and medium shots, which are more behavioral in their expression and don't have to reach that far, still the impulses are the same. The expression for theater is in the same direction as it is for camera work, but it is extended in its physicality, characterization and vocal projection. Once you have a creative technique at your center and the particulars for each medium, it is easy to build the muscle that's needed. It's a matter of practice and experience.

CHAPTER 2

How Transformational Acting Differs from Other Techniques

In order to understand fully how Transformational Acting differs from other techniques, a short review of the evolution of acting methods is helpful.

In the early 1900s, when the great Russian director and teacher Konstantin Stanislavsky developed the system that was to become method acting, he took acting to an entirely new dimension. Prior to Stanislavsky's methods, actors were primarily taught representational acting where they learned to imitate and to master physical and vocal abilities. What came through in a performance was the result of the actor's ability to imitate or pretend.

That changed with Stanislavsky. The new field of psychology was leading to an understanding of human behavior, which had never before been explored. He built on this understanding, teaching the concept of sense memory (sometimes called emotion memory) to attain emotional truth in a performance. This was done by the actor bringing up and re-experiencing memories and sensorial data surrounding an incident in his or her past. Then, by accessing the emotions that accompanied that incident, the actor was taught to transfer them to the character.

Now an actor had the tools to mine the depth of his character by delving into and recreating his own past emotions. For the first time, actors had some real hard-core emotional stuff to work with. This depth of emotional truth brought a new dimension to performances and revolutionized acting. It is this concept of accessing past emotions that is the driving force behind method acting.

Stanislavsky's system also incorporated another new concept: the magic or creative "if," a tool he used to stimulate the actor's imagination. The actor would think about the character and finish thoughts, such as "If I went to a ball, I would wear _____." "If you call me one more time, I will _____." "If I won a million dollars, I would _____." The magic "if" was employed along with the use of scenic structure—asking what when how and where questions, such as "Who am I?" "What do I want?" "What am I doing?" "What time is it?" "What time is it in my life?" "Where am I?" "Where am I coming from?" "Where am I going?" His methods also included objectives, goals, fourth wall and concentration—tools that are still the primary focus of many acting curricula today.

Although Stanislavsky originated sense memory, it was Lee Strasberg who implemented it in New York City at The Actor's Studio. As the story goes, Stella Adler, having returned to New York from a work visit with Stanislavsky, claimed that he himself abandoned the importance of sense memory in later years and focused on action, thru-line, goals, objectives, and super objective.

While it may seem that my technique and Stella's are similar because of her abandoning sense memory, they are really very different. Stella focused more on script analysis, actions, and the character while Transformational Acting works more with the actor's development, uncovering his or her unique self and then finding what is relevant in the material and the character.

In developing Transformational Acting, I wanted to find a way for actors to actually transform who they are, that is, transform their thinking, their approaches, the actions they take and their sensibilities, which result in a rearranged psyche. I also wanted actors to utilize their current emotional vitality within the emotional body.

After having spent so much money and time getting ourselves emotionally, mentally and spiritually cleaned up and balanced, It seemed crazy to bring up all of the past memories we were trying to get rid of. Sense memory forced the actor into mental logistics to help figure out what they thought the character was feeling. The emotions will work on their own. Needing to work up to a moment using sense memory, à la Strasberg, dissipates from the here- and now-ness of the moment. Just as "backloading" with emotion memory is no longer necessary for an actor to have emotions, neither is "frontloading," as with Meisner, in which the actor imagines future events he can then incorporate into the character's emotional aspects.

Just as we have a physical body and a mental body, we also have the emotional body. There, in this inner domain, is your capacity for feelings and desires that have an extended range of emotions far beyond your normal emotional range. Your emotional body is raw emotion.

As I often say, "when you put your hand on a hot radiator, you know exactly how to respond. You don't have to remember back to what pain feels like or to imagine what it will feel like." Your hand is on a hot radiator right now, and that is what your emotional life will be like when using the emotional body.

In that inner domain, when you attune to your emotional

body you are no longer limited to the normal "impulse-response" mechanism that churns out two or three "default" emotions comprising your day-to-day repertory. You access a range of emotions beyond what you have ever felt, like a full orchestra playing notes and melodies beyond its normal repertoire. This allows for a pure interplay and spontaneity, rather than one specific emotion. It also helps you to create the emotional reality of the scene.

In Transformational Acting our preparation uses a Preconditioning Exercise before we work to access our emotional body and inner energy, and then we direct it outward. The exercise takes you to your creative self (from which you access pure creativity) and to your essence (where all of your raw talent, ability, potential, knowingness, fire and uniqueness reside). It also helps you establish where you have come from and gives you a strong opening moment.

Once you tap into your own inner creative self through this approach, you are no longer interpreting the character through your logical left-brain ideas of who the character is. You are instantly creating and allowing the character to inform you. At this point you can open the boundaries of who you know yourself to be and actually begin to transform into THAT character, having a psyche comprised of the character's circumstances, ideas, issues, thoughts and drives. This technique allows you to feel what you are feeling in the moment as you perform a scene, rather than to decide upfront what the character is feeling. You no longer need or want to use larger preplanned blocks of emotions—tirades, so to speak.

In this technique you can figure out a lot of things about the character, such as intention, action, tone and so on, but you do not "figure out" the emotions the character is feeling. Instead, as you are performing, you allow emotions to occur and instinctively express themselves in the moment, with everything that is going on in the present feeding them.

Always start with you. There is nothing but you or like you. You are the creator and the "stuff" that the character is made of.

"Invent yourself as you work."

You are unique. Transformational Acting will help you develop as a person and as a talent, using your uniqueness. Never try to be Meryl Streep, Ed Norton or Tom Hanks. We already have them. They are wonderful. What we don't have is you.

Transformational Acting guides actors into the inner path of their authentic selves.

You *are* unique. Inside of you is your essence. It is home base for you. You live there. Your talent, ability, knowingness, uniqueness and fire are all there. I can't put it there, no one can. You have it. But I can help you find and develop it and continue to keep it growing.

Your creative self is pure, raw creativity, which is the potential through which you give shape to your intentions. When you are in a creative mode, you can tap into the silence and begin to touch and know and utilize this self-substance that runs behind your personality and your thoughts. Through intention, you then bring this rawness into form. You will be brought to a new level of potential through this work But it all begins with you.

Actors achieve brilliant, swift shifts of emotions by tapping into and using the present and immediate full spectrum of emotions that constitute the emotional body. You tap into raw energy, which you then shape and form through the psyche. When you truly experience the character in this way, your audience will also have an experience.

As the technique developed, I used the word PRESENCED to describe the bringing forward of your essence so that you are palpable. When you are "presenced" as an actor, your inner energy is outer-directed and in front of you, so to speak. It is this energy that carries your essence, your light, your charisma and communicates to an audience, whether in person or on camera. Your body contains this presence but does not confine it and so, by turning yourself inside out, your inner energy and your unique self can surface. To be fully presenced, you must first access your creative self and then work from it, rather than from your linear mind. When you are fully presenced in the character and in the moment, you are no longer interpreting the character. You are creating the character.

It is always you. Unfortunately, most actors hide their shyness, craziness, and other points they consider as weaker characteristics. Yet a lot of the characters you audition for today are made up of just the traits you are trying to hide. Is your character hateful of greedy? Guess whose hatred and greed needs to be evoked! Conversely, we humans have far more irregularities than the characters do. Why not give the characters your human frailties and qualities? Directors and producers are looking for such things—they want you to be clear and defined. When you don't allow yourself to be who you are, you rip off your aliveness, your uniqueness, your definition.

In this new context, the words just sit on top of all that is going on. No predetermining; no coloration of words. You are being in the moment and "playing ball."

The basic question I had asked myself was how to get electric, immediate energy into the performances of actors. The new ABCs that follow evolved out of the search for that answer.

CHAPTER 3

The New ABCs and Five Principles

The New ABCs of acting are both contextual and philosophical. They are a new approach to and a new use of yourself, which result in a conscious, ever-evolving life that is in partnership with your creating brilliant acting. You will know you and you will learn the art of transformation in acting. Said more simply, we all know the power of a checklist and this is it.

1. You are, above all, present and presenced. Being presenced means your inner energy is outer-directed and out in front of you, so to speak. This energy carries your essence and charisma and communicates to an audience, whether in person or on camera.

2. You first access your creative self and then work from it rather than from your linear mind. This allows you to be fully presenced.

3. The information about the character, such as circum-

stances, scenic structure, intentions, etc., works you, rather than you working it. Don't act the information.

4. You make 100 percent of yourself available (body, psyche, emotions, sensibilities), so that you can transform those aspects of yourself into character.

5. You allow your impulses to respond naturally, knowing that these responses will eventually alter as the shift into character occurs. Don't jump the gun. (See more on Emotional Body, page 30.)

6. Don't figure out what you think the character is feeling. You feel what you are feeling, not what you think the character should be feeling.

7. Be with and use your particular baseline emotion, the one you would usually run away from such as anger, fear, terror or embarrassment. This baseline emotion is a key to your ability to open up and allow the emotional body to flow.

8. The where, what, who, when structure of the old ABCs is part of Circumstances and Operative Facts. (See Part 3 on Circumstances and Operative Facts, page 84.)

9. The inner self, your essence, your creative self—is your light, your charisma, your shine. The body does not confine it. The body contains it. You learn to allow this energy, filled with your unique self, to surface and to move out ahead of you. It is this inner self that communicates to the other performers and to the audience.

10. Don't try to match what you are feeling to the words.

11. Don't produce. Once you have felt an emotion, trust that it will always be there and don't try to make it happen.

12. Have an experience every time you work. If YOU have an EXPERIENCE, then the audience will have an experience.

Five basic principals emerged from this need to develop these ideas into a technique forming the basis of Transformational Acting:

- Self
- Emotional body
- Psyche
- Character
- Material (working nonobligation to obligation)

Everything that I say from here on falls into one of the 5 categories.

CHAPTER 4

List of Terms Used in Transformational Acting

L et us start with a list of terms, because the language of Transformational Acting is somewhat different from that of other acting techniques, and because the definitions that I give of some of the more recognizable acting terms vary from what is normally taught.

Action Doing (see page 113)

Activity A task: eating, setting the table

Arc Emotional progression that brings you through the entire script

Attention What you focus on

Attitude (see page 79)

Availability Open and responsive

Brilliance Working at 100 percent; get in your partner's face

Choices (see page 108)

Circumstances (see page 84)

Color Don't hold on to one thing, go from emotion to emotion, mood to mood

Communication Make sure that somebody understands what you are saying

Connecting Stay in relationship to your partner no matter what feelings come up

Contradictions Work for opposites

Creative self It is your creative self that enables you to respond spontaneously and intuitively; that frees you of your own circumstances and restrictions; that opens your point of view to new possibilities and unlimited creativity

Desire Let yourself feel what you really desire

Discovery Don't show: discover about relationship, about why you take the actions you take

Dynamics What is really going on under the words?

Emotional body Learn to find, experience and access your emotional substance and currents of energy that add vitality and brilliant, swift shifts to your work

Emotional hook That which you really understand emotionally

Energy Work with very high energy

Essence That which contains your uniqueness, ability, power, talent and fire; your home base; how you recognize yourself underneath your personality, your body structure, your hair cut; a timelessness that is a sense of yourself as a continuum from birth onward into the future

Event The physical event, like the dinner, the wedding

Expressing yourself Don't just do what you think the character should do

5 on 5   Using five lines in five minutes to explore and live in the life of the character using the words only in the truth of the moment

Heightened Performance Extend everyday behavior and gestures

Humanity   Don't judge the character, we all have greed and hatred

Humor   Find it in every situation

Image   Work with the physical design of the character: clothes, accessories

Impulses and Interruption Take out the punctuation (see page 117)

Intention   The inner force that sets you in motion (see page 112)

Interior Monologue   Character's thoughts (see page 55)

Key Line   What the character says that you connect with

Landing/Impacting   Being strong with the other character

Language   How the character speaks

Listening   Really hearing and assimilating

Livingness   The life under the words (see page 37)

Main Action   What the character strives for

Mood   Ambiance

Needs   What the character needs, wants or desires

Nonobligation into Obligation   Work slowly into the obligations of the character circumstances and material

Opening Moments   State and condition the character comes in on, where they have come from

Opposition   Conflicts and obstacles

Passion   Heightened emotion

Physicality The posture and the movements of the character e.g., leaning, twisting in a chair

Playfulness Rehearse as an opera, or a gangster movie

Point of View How the character views the world (see page 78)

Power Go for it; risk

Presenced Bring forth your raw inner self; the energy that contains your essence and distinguishes you, and is immediately sensed on stage, on camera, or in person

Psyche The character's blueprint and how it is organized, comprised of issues, concerns and motivation

Reality How your character holds and defines the events in his life (see page 76)

Relationship Relatedness with two or more people

Relevancy Something in the character, relationships, the material that is pertinent to your current life

Rhythm The amount of movement within tempo

Risk Going beyond what you think you are capable of (see page 64)

Samenesses and Differences How you connect with the character; what is very different between you and the character (see page 82)

Sensibilities Character's reactions, e.g., finicky

Sexuality Getting into the sexual tones of the relationship

Silence The quiet place within yourself where your creativity resides

Situation The psycho-emotional interpretation of an event that the character lives into

State Combination of emotions, circumstances that

creates your state, such as distracted or distraught (see page 106)

Style Being of a period and genre

Subtleties/Nuances Expressing with very little energy, such as subtle behavior

Suspension Not thinking about outcome or results

Tempo Timing

The World The planet your character lives on

Thru-Line The character's journey through the material to get to his or her main action

Tone Angry, confrontational, romantic, suspenseful

Transitions Change of direction or thought

Trust Going in with confidence that you can work all of the moments and challenges as they come to you, just as you do in life

Turning Points Dramatic change in relationship, tone, and action

Vulnerability Being open and surrendered

PART TWO

Accessing Your Essence, The Emotional Body And The Creative Self

Information on Accessing Your Essence, the Emotional Body and the Creative Self

In putting this book together I faced the challenge of teaching you to access your own emotional body as well as assisting you in having an experience of your own essence without my being there. It usually takes a combination of exercises and my ability to recognize and move body energy. But, with proper use of this book, you can be guided to work from your creative self and transform into character while fulfilling the intention of the material. By proper use, I mean that you should do the Preconditioning Exercises set up in this chapter and not just read them.

I begin by teaching you to presence yourself, to access your emotional body and your creative self, which allows your self to freely express.

From this foundation of self we move forward and bring self into situation, which is the psychoemotional level the character responds to. From these responses, an actor organically takes an action, without it being a mental process. Progressing into Livingness the self discovers how much life it can create. We open, extend and transform the self through character work, which includes working with the character's qualities, the transformation of our psyche into that of the character and into the stylistic and cultural factors that shape the character's life. Now the actor/character lives within the material, by way of turning points, and works with the character's intention, thru-line, main action and objective. Risk bookends and gives power to self and the emotional body. Risk gives the self free-dom and power to move into uncharted territory, to play 100 percent, to discover and to be the best it can be. The actor now looks at what his character *can do* versus the common thought: "Oh, they wouldn't do that."

The sequence of lessons allows for the inner energy and cre-ativity to flow continuously and more intensely. Like Fung Shui, it opens inner energy paths through the outer placement of things.

By this progression the actor is guided to have more of an *experience* and less mental gymnastics. It frees the actor while it parallels working from nonobligation to obligation, that is, working with more focus on developing the self than bringing the scene immediately into focus.

Preconditioning Exercise

This particular preconditioning exercise is the one we build our additional preconditioning exercises on. This exercise can greatly benefit you each time you audition or perform. It is designed to allow the creative self to come to the foreground, bringing you forward, presenced and making your emotional body available. This Preconditioning Exercise unhooks you from your daily mental chatter and personal issues. It helps you to steady your focus to the actual moment at hand and bring you to the home base of yourself.

Read through this exercise before doing it. You might want to tape-record the exercise so you can play it back. Or you might ask a friend to guide you through it.

Preconditioning Exercise

1. Close your eyes and allow your creative self to come to the foreground. (When I first began I would imagine an egg breaking, with the halves of shells opening to the right and to the left, while the yellow came to the center.) Use whatever image or feelings come to you. To further help you access the creative self, be aware of the visual sensations you see in your mind's eye. Do you see anything? Do you see nothing? Do you see color? Dots of light? An airplane? A house? What do you see there? Keeping your eyes closed, put your hand over your left eye. While the hand is physically over the eye, what do you see in your mind's eye? Be aware of the feelings these images evoke. Are you calmer, more irritated, and so on? Now put a hand over your right eye and do the same thing. Then go back and put a hand over your left eye again.

2. Now, let's go a little deeper to your essence: who are you underneath your personality, your hair, your weight, your height? What you focus on grows larger, so by focusing on your inner essence you are turning yourself inside out and allowing your inner creative self and your

essence to become prominent. To tap into your essence, see yourself doing something at one year old, then doing something different at 15, at 30, at 50, at 75, at 150. Then see yourself doing something at the age you are now.

3. Now access your emotional body: Put one hand on your heart and the other on your solar plexus. Remember, the emotional body is made up of emotional energy, not a specific emotion. To get more of a sense of that, become aware of trigger points in the body: Touch your hand to any areas that feel sensitive. The sensitive areas might include the throat, the areas a little above or below the clavicle bone (which runs shoulder to shoulder), the solar plexus, the heart, the stomach, the lower stomach, the pelvis, the bony area on your back just below the neck, the back of the head, top of the head, or the face. Now be aware of something beyond you. Hook an imaginary pipeline extending from your sensitive area to something beyond you out into the universe where you feel a yearning, a pulsing, a stirring, a distant calling on a cellular level.

4. Take a breath and inhale. And exhale. And inhale again. Now exhale again—this time to a count of four. At the end of the exhale make a little sound from the pit of your stomach. And now inhale and then exhale with sound.

5. Next, to further distinguish the emotional body and become familiar with it, get a sense of how much it weighs—anywhere from one to ten pounds. Then get a sense of its color. What color is your emotional body?

6. Open your eyes.

These are the fundamentals of the Preconditioning Exercise, which you will add to as it relates to character, or one of the many distinctions that you will be learning. In this way, you will be steadily building on and practicing the Preconditioning Exercise.

LESSON 1

Preconditioning Exercise for the Emotional Body

"You are either controlling or you are powerful."

After doing the Preconditioning Exercise (on page 29), work on a new monologue, one that you have no previous associations with. Do it out loud and conversationally. Don't produce it. Don't color the words. Do not match an emotion to what the words say. Just stay in truth with your real feelings and your nervousness or whatever emotion is driving you. Allow the nerves or emotion to be enveloped by the words. Do not hold onto what you have just discovered about your inner emotions (the emotional core). The feelings will change, making swift shifts, and once again, when they do, let the words envelop the new feelings. All good acting emanates from the area of your body equivalent to a wide stripe down the front including your chest, solar plexus, stomach and not from the mouth.

Because the experience of Transformational Acting is differ-

ent for everyone, throughout this book I'm going to let some of
my students explain the process in their own words.

Don Creech on Working with the Emotional Body

*As Sande says, we carry our own body of emotions around with us
all the time. Your character's feelings can bounce all over the place,
just like your own.*

*My grasp of this proved particularly helpful when I was playing
the roles of Iceman in* The Professional *and Nikolai Rostov on* Law
and Order. *Both roles were typically underwritten in the manner
which allows for the dangerous potential of falling into the trap of becoming one dimensional cartoons.*

*Sande's explanation of the emotional body came as a sort of
epiphany for me and her technique has made all the difference in the
world in my acting.*

LESSON 2

Living in the Situation

"Global metaphors counteract habitual responses."

This is the most difficult lesson you will have. It will feel
as if I am taking you up a ladder to the top of a building
and then pulling the ladder away. YOU KNOW WHAT? I AM!
JUMP!! This risky situation will expand your thinking and

provide you with a solid context for the eight following lessons.

The purpose of our second lesson, "living in the situation," is to show a new way to bring a rich inner life and unplanned behavior to the character. The actor no longer depends solely on the event or the circumstances of the scene for the character's inner life.

Living in the situation means living in the psychoemotional climate of the character, that is, responding psychologically and emotionally to the situation you are living in. Living in the situation is contextual. It is where you are coming from rather than what moves you forward.

To clarify, let's look at what living in the situation is not. I want you to understand that the character's situation is not the circumstances, the story, nor is it the event. The circumstances are the facts that comprise the structure, relationship, character, etc. For example, perhaps the character is an actress; she earns $50,000 a year; it's raining outside; she lives with a friend. These are all circumstances that you embody and which influence what you create. But they are not the situation in which the character is living.

The character's situation is also not the event. The event is the actual encounter, the physical reality for the character. You distinguish the event more easily than the situation because the event is something you handle on the physical level. The event might be a job interview, a wedding, a luncheon or a confrontation.

The situation, however, is the psychoemotional level on which you are living while you are taking care of the physical event. Let's illustrate by using the scene where your character goes to a job interview. The event is the job interview. The circumstances might be a) that you are running late, b) it is raining, and c) the secretary is nasty to you. On one level, you would be handling the physical realities connected to being interviewed: preparing the clothes, doing the research and typing the résumé. BUT YOUR EMOTIONS AND PSYCHE ARE RESPONDING TO THE SITUATION—the psychoemotional trigger (such as the "at-stake-ness") of the job interview.

For each role you play, it is important that you choose a situation you can identify with, one that works for the character and stirs you or is relevant to you as well. This gives you, the actor, the cut-together or ability to blend between yourself and your character.

Living in the situation is contextual, it's where you are coming from versus an action, which is what you are doing. Use a metaphor to describe the situation.

My choices regarding the job interview might be "putting myself into another's hands." Someone else's choice might be "meeting a great challenge" or "taking one's life in his or her own hands." For another, it could be "moving out into the world." In acting, as in real life, the situation is a state which is going on inside of you and may or may not have a direct relevance to the words you are speaking. Yet, your words and behavior are colored by this inner state.

Living in the situation gives the actor a deeper, more relevant psycho/emotional place. Put another way, a situation is using the phrase "what it is" as a prefix to a metaphor: "what it is . . . to want to push the envelope" or "what it is . . . to live at your next level in life" (such as a better job). The actor's job is to find a specific and meaningful situation for the character.

Let's say the actor chooses "what it is to want to push the envelope" for his situation. It has to work for the character in the scene and it has to be relevant for the actor, so it excites him and gets his energy flowing. "What it is to want to push the envelope" can give the actor a strong psychoemotional response, but it must never dictate what the actor feels. It gives the actor the freedom to respond in different ways.

At the job interview the actor might use "what it is to want to please" as his character situation or psychoemotional connection. "What it is to want to please" opens up a myriad of possibilities like being nice one moment, speaking one's mind in another moment, and then perhaps not knowing what to do next. If the situation you choose is "what it is to be living in danger," this opens up many possibilities; for example, being scared, excited, aroused, etc. There is no pre-thinking; it will just happen in the process of living in the situation.

You might even have a conflicting situation, which can set up an attractive dynamic. For example, not wanting to be at the audition but wanting the job; in which case you have to be able to distinguish between your fears and doubts and take action while allowing the conflict to exist. Living in the situation results in spontaneous behavior and emotional vitality. It provides a source of identification with the character. You don't have to be a murderer to identify with the character of a murderer! Working this way gives life and meaning and behavior, which, in turn, will illuminate the words.

An Exercise for Living in the Situation

This exercise allows us to shift our perception from the outer linear world of thought and words to the inner creative world of sensations.

1. Sit in a comfortable chair. Close your eyes. Take a deep breath; fully exhale. Be aware of the sensations that ac-

company the creative self, such as body temperature, body sensations, or inner visual impressions. Work with these visual impressions. What do you see in your mind's eye when you are in your creative space?

2. Now let's become aware of your "essence," which is what makes you special. The "essence" is you without your personality. Your "essence" remains the same, starting at birth and continuing through your life. As an actor you want to identify with this essence rather than with your personality, so you will remain strong and connected to your home base no matter what the character's personality might be. To become familiar with your essence, visualize yourself doing something at eight months old. Now doing something at thirteen years old. Then at twenty years old. At forty. At one hundred. Now go back to sixteen. Lastly, see yourself doing something at the age you are now.

3. Be in touch with the centers of your body that engage the emotional body—the throat, the center of the chest, the heart, the solar plexus, the stomach. Be sensitive to the increased emotional vitality of these centers as they respond to a connection or a yearning or a calling.

4. Bring your attention to the character and start to define the situation in which the character is living. Play with this. Don't restrict yourself by having to make it perfect; you can adjust it as you go. Once you locate a situation that works for the character and is relevant for you, move on to these two questions: When am I like that in life? What does it bring up in me? Do not use emotional words. Rather, describe what it brings up in physical

terms, such as, "I want to run out of the room." Allow the words to sit on top of what is being stirred by the exercise.

Lori Mahl on Living in the Situation

I love "living in the situation" because it gives me an immediate connection to the character and the scene at hand. It hooks me in a very personal way, so I'm free to go out there and live the character's life. When you have that humanity going on, the audience feels it and connects with you.

LESSON 3

Livingness and the Construct of Time

"Follow the life not the words, and the words will fall into place."

My technique diverges from the myth that you must first break the script down into objectives, goals and the subsequent actions that help you to accomplish your objective. We first create as much spontaneous life as possible. This keeps the actor out of their head and into their experience. As for example, in your life when you have the thought, "I need a new jacket" and you go shopping. Life occurs on the way and while you are shopping. It is the same with acting.

Once you develop the muscle of being in action and working from your experience, only then can you be more specific and break material up into beats and actions.

After the complex climb of the previous lesson, this one should be EASY.

Now that you are able to live in a situation, let's look at the premise that the character actually lives 24 hours a day, 365 days a year. The actor starts by extracting the character out of the script, and seeing what his life is like at different intervals during a 24-hour day. He brings what he has found about the character back into the role of the script.

This exercise enables you to create the livingness, the life, the behavior of the character beyond what the script dictates. To reiterate, the script only represents a small portion of the character's life. Once you have created the life, the words lay on top of the life that has been created without any preconceptions about the way they are to be spoken. The life you have created for the character will handle the words.

Lesson 2 mentions the *event* which gives you activities directly related to the current action. But livingness is a way of being, it is not just activities, although activities are a part of it. Livingness develops out of habits, grooming, hobbies, recreation, fixing, touching, moving things, looking for things, being with someone, being in the moment, physicality and so on. Construct of time is one of the key elements in creating livingness. Construct of time defines sections of time, not the physical reality of hours and minutes such as six o'clock or eight o'clock, but "dinner time," "leisure time," "party time," "getting ready for work time," "taking a break time," "getting ready for bed time," etc. When the character lives within the construct of time within a particular scene, the actor is able to generate the physical activity and behavior of the character appropriate to that construct of time.

For a character such as Stanley Kowalski in *A Streetcar Named Desire*, living in "relaxation time" might be having coffee or drinking a beer, playing cards or listening to the radio. The actor's behavior and activities occur in "relaxation time" even though the words of the script might be dealing with something antithetical to relaxation. Your character, for example, might be talking to a friend about making a death threat on someone's life while she is living in relaxation time and polishing her nails.

Another key to livingness is to listen and respond naturally. Do not wait for your cue lines. Become engaged and respond to the actual moment of involvement. If the construct of time for a scene is dressing for a date, the livingness directly related to the scene might be how this character grooms himself and dresses for this date. Livingness not directly related to the scene might be a thought like "Will it snow?" which could lead to the livingness of looking out of the window. Livingness not related to the scene might be wondering "Did I pick up my laundry?" which could lead you to check your wallet and pockets for the laundry receipt.

As we live, the phone rings, the doorbell buzzes, the baby cries, we look out the window to see if the sun is shining, we get a glass of water, we roll up our sleeves. The scene moves in on us. Our character behaves and does his chores and tasks and activities in the unique style associated with that character even though the dialogue might have nothing to do with his livingness.

Commit yourself to building the muscle of spontaneous, imaginative and bold livingness. Do not censor by saying, "My character would not do this." With this kind of thinking, you limit your brilliance. You can always tone your actions down afterwards should you want to. As you push the envelope of actions, your perception will shift and you won't preconceive what you think people will or will not do.

I'm reminded of my first meeting with New York's legendary Mervyn Nelson—producer, film-acting teacher, director, actor. Having heard about me from some mutual students he called to arrange for us to meet. Mervyn came for a late lunch that afternoon. We had our moment of introduction and then he asked me if I was wearing tap shoes. I said that they looked like tap shoes and they really made me feel like tapping. He broke into a time step and then I did a triple time step. Suddenly the new Fred Astaire and Ginger Rogers time-stepped through three thousand square feet of my loft space. After all of the dancing was done, we sat down, ate lunch and began a long friendship. It was livingness at its most spontaneous level. We danced, we talked, we ate, we laughed, I showed him my loft, we became friends.

To connect this anecdote to livingness, I chose "lunch time" for the construct of time.

- Activities for the event—A visit
  - show Mervyn around the loft
  - eat lunch
  - conversation with coffee or tea

- Livingness for construct of time—Lunch
  - tap dancing
  - looking at pictures of actors at our studio who he and I were both working with

The livingness resulted from our relationship and listening to our natural impulses.

To identify the construct of time, do the following Livingness exercise and find what you can do within that time frame.

Livingness Exercise

Do the Preconditioning Exercise (on page 29). Then, with eyes still closed, add the following information from this lesson. Identify the construct of time that your character is living in for the particular scene you are working on. What are some of the things you can do during that period of time? During "getting ready for bed time," can you take vitamins? listen to music? have a cup of tea? read? practice yoga? write in your diary? talk to a friend on the phone? meditate? make lists of your activities for the following day? account for your expenses during the day? And think about future goals?

Think of activities you would not ordinarily think of and see what new activities you can come up with.

Take a moment to imagine a life you can create that is less logical than one you would normally think of. What can your character do during this construct of time that is outrageous, or a bolder choice than you would normally make?

Jim Reynolds on Livingness: How Much Life Can I Create?

Livingness gives me the tools to create the life of the character. It shows up in my body language. It gives me a purpose when I move. It provides me with background reasons for my decisions. As Sande teaches, "The reality will create itself if you are living, on stage, film and TV."

LESSON 4

Character Qualities

*"If you don't see the point to the words, then you don't
have the character."*

Transformation is all about who YOU have to become in
order to transform into that character. All the characters are
within you at some cellular level.

To transform into character you need to make available your
emotional body, your physical body, your mental body (psyche)
and sensibilities, which are used as the raw material for this
transformation. This raw material is then shaped by various
distinctions and exercises we use for character. Although in this
lesson we focus on character qualities, before we go into them,
I want to give you an overview of how we work with character.

We use six character modes, all with their own exercises, to
access character:

1. **Tapping Into:** Tapping into character helps you to find
   the link between you and your character. Suppose your
   morals are different from those of your character, what
   can you tap into, somewhere within yourself, from your
   own bottom line about the *issue* but that also works as
   truth for the character?

   Example: I worked with an actress who was playing a
   character from the Victorian Age. Her character was hesitant to kiss someone. Living in the Victorian Age naturally produced repressed sexuality. It was difficult for the
   actress to relate to her character's sexual responses, so I

suggested she find her own bottom line about sexuality, something she felt she couldn't do. By drawing on her own sexual limits, she was able to come to an inner understanding of the character's response.

2. **Embodying:** Embodying is taking the character into you; sensing the character's essence and energy and allowing it to filter through and be absorbed by you.

   Example: Imagine someone you consider to be a hero, someone who has a certain quality or ability that you would like to have. To embody him, visualize him and feel his energy move into you. Focus on the changes it makes in you. Now do the same thing with the character that you are working on.

3. **Sensations:** What is the sensation—the palpable awareness—that accompanies the character? Notice how the sensations trigger muscular, emotional and physical responses in you.

   Example: Let's say you are all dressed up and going somewhere. If you close your eyes, you can feel yourself do it in a different way. When I am dressed formally, sensations of being at Monte Carlo always hover about. When I am dressed in jeans I have very different sensations. Feel the sensations the character is experiencing.

4. **Sensibilities and Approaches:** The character's sensibilities and approaches relate to his temperament. What is he sensitive to? How does he respond to stimuli? How does he go after what he wants? Find the alignments in taste between you and the character. What is the character drawn to? If a character's sensibilities are nearly as

finicky as mine, that will show up in her approach to sleeping in a strange bed or taking a shower in a strange place. An approach to these sensibilities would be cringing and pulling away. Perhaps the character would bring her own sheets or sleep on top of the bed without taking the bedspread off and covering herself with a coat or a terry-cloth robe. Just as I have done in real life.

5. **Personality and Psyche:** Inner work on your own psyche helps you to embody the character's psyche. This work allows a cut-together or matching up and blending of yourself as you are and as the character needs to be. Personality is then a natural outgrowth of the newly adjusted psyche. This alters your context and the point of view changes. In working with psyche, keep your character's issues and concerns, rather than your own, in the foreground of your mind. (See exercises on Psyche on page 88).

6. **Transforming Your Qualities:** The distinction we will be working with here defines and identifies a character's qualities and then assimilates and uses those qualities to help you transform into character, fusing yourself and the character.

These six modes will assist in your transformation into a new character. Remember, the character lives 24 hours a day. Our work is to discover what the character actually does during those 24 hours and then bring the results discovered into the rehearsal process. Develop your character as fully as possible before you begin to rehearse for theater, for TV or show up on a film set, because this gives the director more to select from. The rehearsal process itself brings more stimuli for transformation, so stay open. A character should be a constantly growing individual just as you are in life.

Through your interplay with the other actors, the rehearsal process gives you the freedom to discover more about your character. You then have the opportunity to work the moments of the play or film script with as much openness and possibility as you can find. Be a risk taker and be willing to let yourself be spontaneous. This technique keeps you working at a level of constantly renewing potential. Playing at risk, you will engage your potential, which, in turn, creates more potential. Your job is to transform into the character. THE ROLE AND THE MATERIAL WILL SHAPE HOW THE CHARACTER LIVES.

Character Qualities Exercise

1. Create a casting notice, such as you might find in a trade publication like *Backstage,* for your character. Example: Joan is a vulnerable, vivacious, slim, happy young mother of two in her mid-30s, but when pressed to the wall shows a strong, aggressive will and hot temper. Joan is given to mood swings but usually can be depended upon for her intelligence, wit and resolve.

2. Choose three of the qualities that represent your character; one quality that contrasts the other two.
   In the character of Joan, the quality, "vulnerable" would be in opposition to aggressive and vivacious.

3. Once you have identified your character's own three qualities, walk around the room keeping yourself open,

receptive and fluid. Keep yourself neutral, like a vessel to be filled or a canvas to be painted.

4. Keeping your character in mind, begin to talk about one of the qualities—just the truth about it, what it brings to your mind. Start each sentence by naming your quality.

   Example: "Aggressive is my quality and aggressive is bold. Aggressive is fast. Aggressive is tough. Aggressive is someone who knows how to deal with a situation and act upon it. Aggressive is nasty/biting/purposeful/etc." Continue filling in the blanks: "Aggressive is _____. Aggressive is _____. Aggressive is _____." Repeat the phrases until you find yourself moving differently and feeling and being different. DON'T PLACE IT, LET IT HAPPEN.

5. Repeat some of the lines of the script, allowing the words to lie on top of how you are now being and feeling.

6. Now, go on to the character's second quality. But don't lose the previous quality as you continue. This is a layering exercise. Layer one quality with its accompanying results on the next quality and so on.

In addition to the qualities this exercise brings up, it gives you new physicality, rhythm, abilities, sensibilities and sensations. Again, always use 100 percent of who you are. Let this exercise work on you and transform you so that you will be cutting together (a blending of you and the character) with the character.

When you work character, the "samenesses" are your emotional connections, the hooks that link you to the character.

Working the "differences"—different occupation, different issues, different qualities, different lifestyle—helps you transform from yourself into that character by going beyond how you know yourself to be.

An exercise on Samenesses and Differences can be found in the Homework section of Part Three on page 82.

Robert Margolis on Qualities Exercise

What was most helpful about using the Qualities Exercise for my role in the TV show Ghost Stories *was that the character emerged organically from my body and not from my head. When I had completed the exercise, I felt more real as the character William than as the character I* THOUGHT *William was. That's what I find most exciting about this exercise and about all of my work with Sande; her technique is always surprising me, always taking me to places that are risky, exciting and truthful. It's a technique that keeps me in a constant state of becoming—both in my acting and in my life.*

LESSON 5

Character Psyche

"We live in a small part of the hologram that we are."

This lesson continues with character at the level of the psyche. The work gives us a better idea of who we have to transform ourselves into. Psyche is how a person is organized; it is a network comprised of issues, concerns, temperaments, drives, motivations, sensibilities, approaches and tastes. One's physicality also develops from the psyche—how one moves, stands, and IS in one's body.

Psyche drives behavior and natural responses, choices, actions and interior monologue. It determines point of view and the way your character perceives, assimilates and responds to stimuli. Psyche distinguishes taste and attraction and defines the personality—why one brother takes the high road and the other the low road. It is a blueprint, which then becomes the master switch.

Psyche dictates:

- Point of view
- World view
- Thought
- Thought structure
- Life experience
- Inner challenges

A good way to understand what is meant by psyche is to spend time with two or three children from the same family and note how each one is different, distinct, and unique despite family likenesses. You can also consider two or three individuals traveling across the country and notice how they are drawn to different routes or modes of travel. Or think of several people doing the same thing—waiters, football players, mothers—the occupation may be identical, but how they approach it and how they do it is unique.

How did you get to be the way you are? Why do certain things bother you? How do you respond to the way things bother you? What attracts your attention? What do you do about going after what you are attracted to?

We could say it's karma or fate but whatever is behind it all, it is the way we are coded, it is in our genes. What we choose to do about and with it is our choice. Choice is the antidote to negative coding.

Questions that begin to program and stimulate the psyche are:

- What type of person speaks like that?
- How does my character deal with anxiety?
- How does my character deal with the world? Is he aggressive, outgoing, shy, laid-back?
- How does my character move through the world? Is he intuitive or calculating?

Remember to search for the opposites: If the character is primarily anxious, when would he be cool, calm and charming?

An Exercise on Psyche: The Party Exercise

1. Do the Preconditioning Exercise (on page 29) to bring your creative self to the foreground.

2. Keeping your eyes closed, see your character walk into a party where it seems fitting for him or her to be. Be specific, let the character dictate. Is it an uptown cocktail party? Are there violins playing? Is it a midtown bash? Is there a DJ? Are you at an East Village party on pillows having a psychic reading? Is it at a house in the Holly-

wood Hills? At Malibu Beach? Describe the music (if there is music) and the sounds. As the character enters the room, be aware of what he is thinking. Does he feel adequate? Shy? Attractive? Excited to be there? Is the character comfortable in what he is wearing? Does he want to leave?

3. Walk further into the room and begin to talk with someone specific—someone the character wants to know.

4. Now a person walks by with hot coffee and spills it on your character. Respond immediately! Was the character's response different from how you usually respond?

Note: From this exercise you learn a lot about your character's psyche because it allows you to experience how the character responds differently than you would.

Tripp Hanson on Psyche

The thing about this technique that I find intriguing is its practical application. With other techniques, I'd get "tied up" in my thoughts ABOUT technique, as opposed to having something I could actually USE.

While working on a role for Crazy for You, *what I discovered when I tapped into the psyche of this character was a great deal more than I would've thought to "invent." The process became very rich for me, as opposed to fulfilling some staging and pretending some cardboard actions! I created a living human being.*

Good thing, because I did the Broadway show for two and a half years—over 850 times!

LESSON 6

Stylistic And Cultural Factors

"As an actor you have the ability to temporarily
transform your life, your lifestyle, what you wear, what
you speak, and, of course, how you think. This brings you
into the life, thoughts, and lifestyle of your character.
Wake up—to the world around you!"

You and your character are part and parcel of the style and culture of the time you live in, just as I have been greatly influenced by the decades of the 1960s, 70s, 80s, 90s and the new century.

Stylistic and cultural factors are the physical outer embodiment of the character's inner psyche. These factors influence how the psyche shows up in life. This happens through lifestyle choices—where you go, what you do, how you dress, and the other choices you make. It also occurs through worldly cultural factors such as the music you hear, the economic conditions of the world, the political picture and so on. This embodiment will show up in your personality and physical appearance as well as being brought into the play or film script.

Stylistic factors create a profile of the culture (your group of peers) and the style of the character. It may take some research to understand all of these factors. Even if the event takes place "today," "today" is different than it would have been a few years ago and than it will be a few years from now. You want to look at the factors, such as, "Who are they?" "What do they look like?" "How do they live?" Then, apply these factors specifically to the character.

Answer the following questions regarding the stylistic factors surrounding the character's lifestyle. Do this first for yourself and then for your character, which will pinpoint the differences between you and the character.

1. What is your occupation? Economic bracket?

2. What places do you frequent? Where do you hang out? What restaurants do you go to?

3. Where do you shop? At big stores? Boutiques? What kind of clothes do you buy? Are they trendy? Classy?

4. What kind of food do you eat? Are you a vegetarian?

5. What is your language? What slang do you use? How do you phrase words? How do you speak?

6. Where do you go for entertainment? Do you stay at home in front of the television or go out dancing? Do you go to the symphony and the theater? What kinds of plays or music or lectures would interest this character?

7. What are the customs, social mores and morals of the character?

Note: On page 88 there is a more advanced lesson on Psyche where you actually transform your own psyche into that of the character.

Let's look at the cultural factors that influence the character. What "world" does he live in?

1. What period of time is the character living in? What are the facts about the time period itself? If it's the 1930s, the facts include, the Depression and the beginnings of wartime. Create a catch phrase for yourself for that period of time, like, "Hang tough for America." If it's the 1980s, your catch phrase might be "Take it over the top." Be very specific. You definitely have to do research if you are working on a period piece. There is a vast difference between the 60s, 70s, 80s, 90s and early years of the new century. Please do not run them together.

2. What is the truth about the part of the world you live in geographically, economically, socially?

3. What is the prevailing ideology of the day? What's the political picture? Who is the President? Prime Minister? King, Queen or leader?

4. What is the economy of the world? Of your particular character?

5. Who are the painters, trendsetters, architects, composers and musicians who are creating the ambiance and mood of that time?

6. What is your character's philosophy regarding all of this?

All of the above are stimuli that you respond to. They affect who you are at a given period of time in your character's life.

One of the fun parts of acting is being able to live in many different lifestyles and learn about other cultures. Right now, think of another occupation you'd like to have. Allow your imagination to play with the lifestyle that this occupation would lend itself to.

Exercise on Stylistic and Cultural Factors

1. Do the Preconditioning Exercise (on page 29) and allow the creative self to come to the foreground.

2. Begin to talk about the time and the period your character lives in. Include anything you know about it. Go through the preceeding lists of stylistic and cultural factors and answer how they relate to your character.

3. Do some research on stylistic and cultural factors. A good book for this is *Panati's Parade of Fads, Follies and Manias* by Charles Panati. Find clothes and other essentials relating to the character. Go to a restaurant or an event that the character would actually go to. As always, remember that the character lives 24 hours a day; your homework can be as simple as taking your character out to buy a newspaper.

Your imagination should be fueled by now.

Use the internet, which is a glorious resource for information. But do not ignore museums, art galleries, special exhibits and books. Art books are a wonderful resource for defining periods of time. Outside research provides the social contact that has gotten lost with the advent of the computer. Get out of your apartments and houses!

Robert Fowler on Stylistic and Cultural Factors

While working on The Producers, *which takes place in 1959, I immersed myself in Sande's technique of Stylistic and Cultural Factors: the period of time, the fervent political arena, the opposing cultural factors.*

Sande has taught me to acknowledge everything that is going on for me and turn it over to the role. It helps me create the world of the play yet allows for my personal daily differences. I can be living in a different era using my experiences of the current moment.

LESSON 7

Interior Monologue

"Put your own crazy into the character."

Interior monologue is our ongoing inner dialogue, the mental chatter that seems to have a life of its own and can drive us crazy. Characters have an inner dialogue composed of their own issues. Your personal issues, stimulated by the material, can also be used. Many things stimulate the interior monologue that is a bridge between you and the character.

Try this exercise as you begin to work on the script alone. Go through it with your own actual thoughts and then complete it as the character you are working on.

Example: Suppose you are playing Stella in *A Streetcar Named Desire*. Your own thoughts are "I'm really afraid." Now, express that thought but complete it with the character's thought: "I'm really afraid—if I side with my sister, Stanley might leave."

Interior monologue can also be provoked by working with the character's issues, drives and concerns. When working a character's interior monologue, our own thoughts, issues and concerns may be running through our mind, but it is important for you to focus on the issues and concerns of the character—not on your own. Take notice of the character's wonderings, musings and questions. As you transform into the character, their thoughts will inform you.

The aspect of interior monologue this lesson works with is how the script dialogue moves in on you and stimulates your interior monologue, to cause you to want to interrupt rather than wait from cue to cue.

Cue to cue is not how real people engage in a conversation, or think. We do not talk or think according to punctuation. By the way, coming to work today I heard of a place that sells, at half price, Armani suits for men and women. Before I finish you will be thinking where? HOW do I get them? You would not wait until I completed what I was saying. It's the same with acting. When you are really listening and being with someone, you naturally respond to what interests you.

Interior monologue keeps you very much in the moment. It is the thread that connects turning point to turning point and transition to transition. It also keeps you motivated and connected as you move from place to place. It is very useful when actors are involved in technical maneuvers while they are performing in a big Broadway musical.

Note that I am not suggesting you plan an interior monologue. An interior monologue should be fresh and inspired. You must, however, know the character's issues and concerns to stimulate your interior monologue. What you think, you become.

Interior Monologue Exercise

Invite a friend—another actor is best—to dinner and work together on these exercises. You can team up as buddies working on each other's material. A friend who has not acted, though, but is intrigued by the process might enjoy reading with you. Begin to run your lines and verbalize your actual interior monologue in answer to the other actor's lines. Then follow through with the words in the script. Eventually you will be expressing your own thoughts fluidly while using the actual material.

Ginger Prince on Interior Monologue

Sande's interior monologue exercises made me a continual work in progress. You never stop listening or learning. So many people asked me, "Don't you get confused on stage when you know BOTH characters' lines but are only playing one," as I did in the original off-Broadway production of Steel Magnolias? *With Sande's training that simply didn't happen. Interior monologue led me to the sensibilities, thoughts and actions of two totally different living, breathing human beings.*

Turning Points And Transitions

"There are many turning points in life; you know as they are occurring that your life will never be the same. Since life on stage or film or television can be a condensed version of actual life, we as actors have to be sensitized to go through a number of turning points in a short period of time."

Our focus moves now from character to the material. Remember to bring all that you've learned so far into your work.

Turning points provide the orchestration and the emotional outbursts in the scene. Emotional thoughts lead to turning points while mental thoughts lead to transitions. For example, an emotional thought might be "I hate you!" or "Get out of here!" A mental thought might be "Well, let's go out to dinner and think about this later." Both create change. Turning points explode the material while transitions segue.

Turning points are related to the material. Whenever you discover change, have a conflict, lose or win, or have a new understanding—there is a turning point. Something is new—different than it was before. You feel a change of tone, mood, emotional impact or your behavior.

A turning point for Stella in *A Streetcar Named Desire* is when Blanche arrives. A turning point for Blanche is when she realizes that her sister loves Stanley. Turning points result in taking different actions, changing the mood, altering your approach or changing the tone. You have to frame that change. It is not enough just to feel it, the audience has to see it—without you showing it. The audience has to see your discovery and what you're going through—physicalization for theater and behavior for film.

Example: For theater Blanche might begin to pack and then, realizing she has nowhere to go, fling the clothes out and slam the suitcase shut. For film, she might just take one article of clothing and slowly sit, holding it against her face. Then again, she might choose not be active and allow her mood to reflect her feelings.

Look at how intense changes affect your life. Most of us make a big deal of going through life changes. Take a moment and think of the last three changes in your life. Not only was it big for you, but everyone close to you was probably affected. Eventually, you got into action and went with the change. Soon enough, whatever changed became the status quo.

At every turning point there is a new octave which escalates and intensifies the material. It might require being more subtle but the important thing is, it is more specific and defined. So ... TURNING POINTS EQUAL CHANGE. At the moment of change the level of energy, relatedness and "at-stake-ness" spirals up to a new octave.

Think of interplay between actors as actually playing ball. When you are not sensitive to the change and not listening, the ball drops. (Does that sound familiar? Do you recognize it from your life?)

Turning points are the motor for the thru-line. It keeps the tension between the actors in line. Do not let the ball drop. Keep the image of the ballgame while the momentum grows and you will continually play a bigger game.

Both transitions and turning points provide orchestrations and changes. Transitions, however, are more subtle than turning points. A transition is going from one phase to another, one movement to another, one idea to another, one mood to another, or one thought to another. A transition is moving from the present to the future.

Listening connects you to what's going on. What are you listening for? What is the need that's not being fulfilled?

For an actor, a transition can add insight to the inner map of the character. It makes us aware of why characters change subjects, what things they don't want to face, what things they are anxious to do Do not focus on transitions for an audition, use them for rehearsal. It is turning points that add more excitement and more drama to a scene and performance.

Exercise on Turning Points

1. Do the Preconditioning Exercise (on page 29). Take a breath and let your creative self come to the foreground.

2. Be aware of the sensations that accompany your character. These can be the sensations of class, of mood, of being in a specific place, of a different period of time. Just let them evoke in your cellular memory a feeling of familiarity that you have with the character. As the feeling fills you, adjust your body a little bit to accommodate a new physical frame, a new rhythm, a new psyche.

3. In your mind's eye take a look at a section of the scene that you are working on. Look at the changes in it. How do you feel at that change? What's different at that change? What do you want to do at that change?

4. Allow this experience to sensitize you to change. Notice the change in your own life and how you respond.

Nikita Ager on Turning Points

I played a sweet Southern girl in the TV series Providence. *The first turning point came when she had to become a stripper. Sande helped me to bring up that darker side of myself for the character. The second turning point was when she took control of her life saying good-bye to stripping and to the bad guy she was in a relationship with. Here Sande helped me to find that organic need and power within myself that took the character into a different phase of her life.*

LESSON 9

Intention And Action

"We learn in particles; intention organizes it."

This lesson focuses on the script, rather than on the character. Let's look at the character's intention and how action results from that intention. The intention is what the character is going for and the way in which he's going for it. It comes from his desire. Intention gives us the fuel to fulfill our goals.

Look at the body of the material, for the character's "thru-line"—the character's journey. The thru-line is how this person travels through or lives life in the entire script. We see how a character progresses from the beginning to the end of the script and attains his goals and fulfills his overall objective. Every scene has an objective with its own intentions. Intention is what motivates the characters to fulfill their goals; the force that keeps you out in the field.

When I speak of intention, a vivid example that comes to mind occurred when I was directing *The Insect Comedy*. The evening after my first day of casting, my bell rang and a man introduced himself as Bill Sanderson. He asked if he could read for me. I snapped back, "No! This is my home and auditions ended at 5pm." For the next half-hour the bell rang on and off. Bill pleaded, asked, insisted. He tried everything to get me to hear him read. From the lobby I could see him on a TV monitor. He wanted to audition for the part of The Tramp; he felt he was It. Bill continued, "Just give me a chance. I'll do a great job for you." My anger at having my privacy invaded melted when he said that. I let him up, he read and was exceptional and got the job there and then. It was Bill's intention and ability to take action that is exemplified here. There is a difference between what Bill did and brash pushiness. His actions came from the heart. He knew he was the right guy and that the part belonged to him. It was so true, that he went right into the role of the tramp on the Bob Newhart TV series.

Exercise on Intention and Action

To work intention for the character, you must first stimulate your own "intended-ness," the center of our intentions.

To do that, choose a command that is important to you the actor (NOT the character), one that resonates with you. Call it out. For example, "Get out of here!" "Help me!" "Stop doing that!" Then locate a command relevant for your character and call that out. Now locate your character's intention and a few of the actions that will help fulfill that intention. If your character, for example, wants to be at the top of her field, her intention will fuel her desire and commitments. Her command might be "Give me that!" or "Hire me." One action might be to form a relationship with everyone she meets who can help her. Subsequent actions to help fulfill this might be to send flowers to people, invite them out to dinner, send birthday and holiday cards. Later, when you are rehearsing or performing, continue to work the actions. This distinction is as effective for living our lives as it is for working the material.

Adam Rapp on Intention and Action

During rehearsals and rewrites for my play Netherbones, which was commissioned as the inaugural play at Steppenwolf Theater's 1995–96 New Plays Lab. I kept running into the snag of what Hume, the main character, could do. Do, do, do I kept thinking. As an actor I superimposed myself onto Hume. I thought about the things around me: the kitchen table, the countertops, the party hats, the confetti flying about. Then it came to me. It was like one of those rare moments of suspension that you experience as an actor when an action seems to come from some dark pocket of chaos inside of you. It occurs suddenly and irrevocably. It's part risk and part surrender. It's not having notions about what your body might do. It's allowing the current of the scene to fully inhabit you. It's a feeling I had been experiencing as an actor during my scenes at Sande's studio. And it was the first time I had applied this philosophy to my work as a playwright.

Taking Risks

"Risk creates a new chemical balance. It is exhilarating. It gets you to take chances. You fly."

What do most actors want? To be bold, to be dangerous, to work on the edge, to be connected. What interferes with this? Holding onto pictures, figuring things out, controlling how you respond, rehearsing and then trying to repeat the exact emotions. Cut it out!!

Repeat the blocking and staging. Hit the marks, each and every take. Know your lines. Let everything else—emotional life, behavioral response, relationship and interior monologue—occur in the moment. Don't freeze your performance.

The *have-tos* are learnable and become part of your kinetic sense. When you enter a room in your house, you automatically (through kinetic sense) know where the light switch is. Similarly, with training and experience, the technical aspects become second nature so that you can work in the moment and take risks.

Some of the technical have-tos for film work are hitting marks, where to look, how to work within a frame, knowing which camera is picking you up, and how to work for a camera at various distances. These are not haphazard. For theater, they include projecting, knowing how to communicate to others, being visible to the audience and allowing your inner truths to show up visually with a sense of heightened performance. Then your ability to take risks will put you up-front; it will make you highly visible and distinguish you.

If you want to be a dangerous, risky actor, take chances and be risky. Live in some danger. Be willing not to know. Become engaged and have an experience; that's the only way the audience will have an experience. In short, take the lid off. Risk is how you work with potential and create more potential.

But, don't do your homework out there. Don't do Preconditioning Exercises out there. Get into relationship and play ball. That's it. In life, you handle problems and concerns as they occur. For creative work it's the same; you handle it bit by bit and moment by moment. This allows you to take risks.

Open yourself up, listen and respond. An actor who trusts himself is risky.

Anthony Rapp on Risk and Daring Yourself

Of the many distinctions I've been working with since I first started studying with Sande in 1990, the work we've done on taking risks has always thrilled me. As far as I can tell, having a willingness to risk it all, to go outside your boundaries, is paramount to being any kind of artist, but it's essential for an actor, since acting is a living, breathing form. Risk, as we discuss it, means letting go of any and all of your preconceived notions and concerns and allowing yourself, in fact, daring yourself, to be open and alive and electric and sur-

prising. It's the key to being in touch with any experience of real creativity.

When I was appearing in Rent, *I was the narrator and therefore, in some ways, the center of the show. I had started out in musical theater as a child, but all of my work as an adult had been dramatic. I hadn't been in a musical for many years when I got the call to audition for* Rent. *Of course, I was excited, but I was also a little doubtful of my prospects. I certainly had fears about my voice. I hadn't sung in a show for so long, would I still have what it takes? And although I had harbored secret fantasies of being in a rock band, I hadn't thought I would really be the type who would be taken seriously singing that kind of music. So I knew that, in order for me to have any chance at being a part of this show, I would have to set all of those concerns aside and just go in and sing my heart out and risk it all. And I did just that and, well, the rest, as they say, is history . . .*

In working on this role, I stayed in the moment and allowed the experience of being with the ensemble to shape me. I went through all of the crises they were going through and explored my own life in a way that correlated with the issues in the show. Through this work I was able to do my part in creating the ensemble as the close knit family they became.

Sande Shurin on Inappropriate Risk

A word of caution on risk: I was at Actor's Equity auditioning a male principal for a Broadway show I was directing. The actor entered and began his audition. He jumped onto a chair and started stripping as he spoke. I called out that that was enough, Stop! The stage manager wrestled him off the chair. We finally quieted him down and got him out of the audition room. This actor had operated

out of shock tactics. His inappropriate approach made him some-
one I would not remember for another role. He may have risked,
but you must weigh risking and appropriateness; even then you
may sometimes lose but you leave yourself open to so much
possibility.

You must find the criterion for appropriateness from within,
while at the same time keeping your eye on the effect your behavior
is having on the people around you. If you review the Bill Sander-
son episode on page 62, you will see I sensed he was persistent but
speaking from the heart, and he sensed I sensed that. There is a fine
line and, as with everything else, you must go by your instincts.

PART THREE

How To Use This Technique

Homework
Preparing Rehearsal

You need to begin your work before you go to an audition or a rehearsal; it is your HOME-work. Then, when you are actually shooting a film or rehearsing a play, you have already begun to transform into character. Doing homework helps you bring in enough choices for the director to select from. With the advantage of having done this work beforehand, you can put all of your attention on the interplay between you and the people you are working with.

Rather than pulling the play apart intellectually, allow your work with the material to be "experiential." Your first read-through should be for the experience you get; how it stirs you emotionally and imaginatively. Follow the inner connections that take place. On subsequent readings, look at sections of the material noting changes, intention, actions and objectives. Get a good sense of the relationships. Look for changes in mood, tone, turning points. List key circumstances, pertinent and operative facts. Let your mind go from the literal circumstances to the nonliteral, imaginative data that it brings up in you.

Homework will help you transform into another human being and live in a new reality with a new identity created by a

71

new psyche. It will give you a different impulse and emotional response system and will help you absorb a whole new set of circumstances and stimuli. IT IS OPENING THE HOLOGRAM OF WHO YOU ARE TO INCLUDE WHO YOU CAN POTENTIALLY BE.

When I talk about character transformation, I often use this as an example: Let's say I took you to the French Riviera and gave you a fishing boat with which to earn your living. Who would YOU have to become to do that? For me, A New York Princess, working on a fishing boat would be a huge stretch. More then just changing lifestyle would be needed for me. I would have to change my belief systems, ingrained habits, values and sensibilities before I could earn my living on a fishing boat. What would it take for ME to do that?

The psyche is the master switch in transformation. It is like software to a computer. By changing software we change the process. Similarly, when the program is changed in the psyche it gives the character a new thought process and emotional response repertoire. I want to drive home, that technique (a work system) is the easy side of training an actor. Working with the technique on distinctions, such as point of view, intention, objectives, main action and thru-line, though imperative, is easier than working on the actor's inner system: fears, anxieties, habitual responses. These elements are in opposition to the actor's being presenced. The emotional body and psyche are part of a reconfiguration, which is about opening yourself up so you can use all of who you are and bring your own vulnerability into the work.

Transformational Acting is a rigorous but ultimately exhilarating challenge. You must keep working at building new muscle so you can continually push yourself to the edge. When you have an experience, as I've said before, the audience will also have an experience.

As actors we need to trust ourselves, to be in the moment and respond as we really feel. It's not about figuring out what we should be feeling or who we should be. This body of work includes working on your self, on character and on learning new distinctions. It is a step-by-step guide for developing your personal homework technique and preparing for auditions. It also gives you an approach and a focus for the actual rehearsal process and for working with a director. Learning this technique is working with the spirit, the soul and the heart.

The exercises that follow are part of the homework system. Keep a diary from the first read-through of each project. Notate whatever comes up for you while doing the exercises. Record relevant dreams, attractions and encounters. Once your creative pre-conscious is in gear, synchronicity seems to occur.

5 on 5

The purpose of this exercise is to utilize 5 lines in 5 minutes. Our creative spirit does best when it has the freedom to explore, to find, to create, outside the obligations of the material or the character.

Exercise

For this exercise only, you will need a partner. Perhaps you can find another actor, or a friend, to work with. Work the scene from the material, without words. Do not mime or improvise. Live the moments and explore the relationship. When it feels absolutely necessary to say a line do so. If the actor you are working with does not have the need to respond sequentially, they will speak at some point when the moment is there for them.

Slowly add the structure and obligations of the scene and the character. By this time you will have found a lot of the life and sub-text underneath the words.

Speak only when the moment generates the thought.

Character

"What I call transforming into character is a transformation into the deepest and highest parts of yourself."

Considering life's complexities and the challenges for humanity, we need a new take on the characters we create.

Our characters are too simplistic, we must go deeper and reveal more. We need to express emotions, concerns and issues that usually exist on a less aware level for us and we have to learn to express more intensely.

Take a truthful look at the characters you see in any medium. What engages *you*? What makes a difference to you? Television brings us amazing interviews and stories from real people. TV talk shows reveal the most intimate details of people's lives.

The route into this newest wave of acting begins with the

use of yourself and then character. The characters you create need to be richer and extremely real in their humanity even if the style is surreal. Set them up with more contradictions; use extremely opposing forces. Your character can, for instance, be off the wall, grounded, wellbred, eclectic *and* bohemian all at the same time.

Actors are aware of being a vehicle for the subtext, but now we will have to know more about our characters, as well as ourselves, so that we can express the supra-text (the character's personal feelings expressed) as well as the subtext (feelings that are not expressed verbally).

The following exercise will give you some insights into creating a more complex character.

First do the pre-conditioning exercise on page 29. Then:

- Speak aloud about how you perceive your character's qualities on first reading
- Allow 10 contradictions to come to your mind
- List 10 secrets that your character would not mind if people knew; they are just not obvious
- List 3 secrets the character would not want anyone to know
- What is your character's occupation?
- What other jobs would your character like to try?
- What is your character's education?
- Think of a longing your character has
- Add a circumstance
- Get an opposite circumstance
- Think of your character's strangest phobias
- What terrifies the character?
- Is there something your character doesn't like to know about herself?

As you work with this exercise, notice what is changing in you, what you are actually bringing up in you. Later exercises in this section will help you transform into the character you have just put together.

Reality, Point of View and Attitude

One of the most potent keys to entering an actor's system is to have him expand his reality. Most of us hold on tightly to our reality and points of view and actually defend them, which makes it very difficult to enter a new reality for the character. We bring our preset perceptions and ideas with us, rather than expanding to encompass those of others. Think of people buying a new house to expand—perhaps have a garden or a larger dining room—and then, instead of expanding into it, they try to keep it the same by bringing along all of their old furniture, even though a lot of it won't work or fit. We try to feel safe. We dig in with our feet and hold.

Reality

Each character has a very intense reality. If you work a scene from your own reality you get you. By changing your reality you penetrate the character's life.

Example: let's look at the reality of bike messengers. Here in Manhattan they whiz past pedestrians, clearly angry at them for being in their way. Messengers on bikes appear not to see or understand the idea of green lights and red lights. People are in their way—period. To keep to their schedules, if necessary, they run you down. Delivering or picking up packages is their only reality. My reality as a pedestrian is that they are irresponsible, dangerous and nasty. Two totally different perspectives. To help you penetrate your character's reality, try the the next exercise, especially if it is far from your own.

Reality Exercise

Examples of topics to talk about:

- World Trade Center Bombing
- Relationships
- Your new job

Treat this exercise like jumping off a diving board. You want to keep the risk factor alive. Just talk. Make up a story, not related to your script, like one of the topics referred to above. Dive in and speak as if you really know what you are talking about. If you work with a partner, have him ask you some short questions, such as "Where were you at the time of the bombing?" "What were you doing at the time?" If you are working alone, try looking into a mirror while doing this exercise.

Continue until it has a real ring for you, then move on to a topic from your script that you would like to know more about. If you are not a parent and your character is, speak about your children. It takes boldness to enter another's reality. Be as inventive as you can. Let inventiveness take you along. Your reality shifts in a moment when you stop holding onto it for your identity.

Point of View

Looking at the character's point of view, we see it is intertwined with their reality; actually, it comes out of having that reality. We hold our reality intact and defend it with our point of view. It is made up of our beliefs and philosophies. In *A Streetcar Named Desire*, Stanley Kowalski's point of view is that of "Top Dog," "A guy who calls all the shots" or "King of the hill." Look at how he carries it in the full spectrum of his life, no matter where he goes. He brings his point of view with him into every scene.

Point of View Exercise

First speak about your own personal point of view on an issue contained in the script.

Now do the same for your character for the same issue. As you do this, allow your point of view to give way to the character's. Character actions will come out of the character's point of view and these actions take on an ease when they are firmly established in the point of view. After all, we do what we believe. Some of Stanley's actions are, for example, coming and going as he pleases and monopolizing the household.

Note: You might also want to go back to the Exercise on Psyche in Lesson 5 to help determine what it is about the character that motivates his point of view.

> *"Stop hiding out! A performer has*
> *the responsibility to be visible."*

Attitude

Attitude is point of view brought to its epitome and expressed through the body. It is best used for theater where the physicalization and characterization need to be visible in a larger house. For close-up and medium shots on camera, point of view is preferable.

As a society we are able to embrace attitude. We have plenty of it. Actors have this great gift of being able to use what we're already very good at in the service of the character.

Exercise on Attitude

Work through this exercise while standing. This exercise will extend Point of View into an Attitude Phrase.

- Find a repeatable phrase or sentence based on your character's point of view.
- From his point of view, you might choose Stanley's sentence, "I don't like what's going on here."
- Continue to repeat the phrase or sentence. As it moves through the body, allow it to extend and grow larger and more adamant. Stanley's sentence might become "Show me respect."
- Include a behavioral action at the end of the sentence, such as, pointing a finger, thus creating your attitude phrase.

Attitude is a physicalization of point of view. It is used to advantage in theater. Point of view is very subtle, often reflected in your thinking and your mood, which is perfect for the camera.

Character Homework

As we progress with character, we use a 5-step process:

1. The truth of YOU: This process begins by being aware of what is really going on for you. Are you annoyed? Warm? And so on.

2. Pack a bag: Actors come into class daily, looking like they are ready for the airport: duffel bags, suitcases on wheels, and backpacks, as well as their handbags and briefcases. It always surprises me to find that this is for his or her daily work, audition, rehearsal, class, socializing day and evening. Prepare a version (can be smaller) for your character. Pack whatever they would put into their pockets, pack for the day. Include unique objects and paraphernalia. Do not censor or be concerned where or how items fit into your character's life. Allow yourself to be drawn to these items and apparel.

3. How do you take an intuitive step into the character?: This needs to be an instinctive, creative process. You may find the door by stepping into the character's psychological makeup—wanting to be left alone or on the other

hand, wanting to fit in. It can also be inspired physically, such as intuitively choosing a pair of white kid gloves while playing the role of Jacqueline Kennedy, supervising her children as they eat candy and play with crayons.

4. Truth for the characters: First extend yourself to their truth. What is their life like? Where are they going? What are they up to? Use their circumstances to help you find what is true for them.

5. Relevant to you: What is relevant and meaningful to you, now, in your life; about the character, their situation, their issues, their relationships, how they go about life. **Never work on anything until you make it relevant to yourself.**

A big question to be answered by you is, if I were working on this role for a year what would I be working out or examining in my life? If you were working on *True West,* might you be examining how you relate to your own brother or mother? Could this bring up feelings on how you were treated as a child? Might it touch on guilt about having a better life than your sibling? You must examine how this affects your relationships in the present.

Character Exercise

You will need a pencil and paper for this exercise. Write in a 3-column format as shown below. For this and the following exercise, Circumstances and Operative Facts, I have used a fictitious character.

You will be looking at the "samenesses" between you and the character. Samenesses give you emotional connections with the character, always use what is true, what you have in common. This is how you cut together or "splice" yourself with the character. You will look at the "differences" between you and the character too. A difference is the spark that ignites the transformation. It is where creating begins. You may also use the Preconditioning and Qualities exercises as well as Psyche work and research, to help with this.

Look at the third column as something you have given away, not developed, detached from, disregarded or not had the opportunity to experience yet. The further you go from yourself the more you meet yourself.

SAMENESSES	GRAY AREA	DIFFERENCES
Always begin with what you bring to the role that works in alignment with the character. Use strong points, such as your charm, and darker ones, such as your nastiness.	Bring some of your qualities to the foreground that usually lurk in the background and are seen only now and then. (Because I'm aggressive, bold, and outspoken, you wouldn't immediately call me an overly tender person. But just watch me with my cats—I'm as tender as they come.)	Identify the differences between you and the character. This is where the creation begins, where you have to think of character issues, concerns, lifestyles, occupations and approaches. What do you have to shift within you to become this way? What does the character have or do that would enrich you tremendously and help you to grow and transform? This question will help you make the transformation into a character who is not immediately apparent to you.

The Character Exercise, using a politician as an example.

SAMENESSES	GRAY AREA	DIFFERENCES
I have lots of samenesses with this character:	A politician would have a certain adaptability, like shaking hands and kissing babies.	Politicians are always alert, able to be affable and create value at morning meetings.
A leader		
caring about certain issues politically, like no death penalty, health care	I'm not one for social amenities.	I'm most often up early, but in my own frame of mind, thinking, creating, working, phone coaching, meditating. Yes, I have worked with others in the early morning, but I'd rather not.
I've appeared on TV, radio, lecture halls—in public.	It annoys me when randomly asked, "Hi, how are you?"	
	But I can reach into myself and bring this ability to the foreground. I can be engaging and know how to be available and charming.	Being a politician and doing it seriously and with enjoyment would have a huge impact on my life and probably bring me to a whole new level in my career.
	It's just a well-motivated shift in perception.	In developing this character, I might try a power breakfast support group with some friends, at which my goal would be to create value in their lives. It might take more than one breakfast. At these breakfasts, I would notice what comes to the foreground that I could use for the character. For me this would be an extreme way, but very potent.

Circumstances and Operative Facts

Circumstances are operative facts fed into scenic structure. Who am I? What time is it in the play? In my life? What am I doing? When is it? Where am I coming from? Where am I going?

Circumstances and Operative Facts can be related to character relationship, occupation, period of time. Circumstances are the facts that generate the scene, that put you into action, and that help you make your Choices.

Circumstances and Operative Facts Exercise

This is a *written* 4-column exercise.

OPERATIVE FACT (All of the pertinent literal data)	WHAT DOES THE OPERATIVE FACT MEAN TO ME? (The state it puts me into)	ILLITERAL CONNECTIONS (Such as, imagination, dreams, intuition, serendipitous meetings)	HOW DOES IT SHOW UP IN THE MATERIAL (Choices)
Always use a circumstance that you relate to. The character is a director	Powerful Certain Decisive	The character meets a playwright who is looking for a director (An example of a serendipitous event)	The character is constantly taking notes and looking through pictures and résumés

The Calendar

J ust as you keep a date book, keep one for your character.

Calendar Exercise

To represent a month of a date book, prepare an appointment calendar for your character by drawing a grid on an 8½ x 11 inch sheet of paper, to cover a month in the life of the character. Divide each day's square so you will have room to get about 12 appointments on each day. You'll have to abbreviate. (See example on page 86)

Focus on the character's occupation. What time does the character get up in the morning? What time does he go to work? Firstly, use circumstances from the script, then use your imagination to embellish the actual circumstances and events. Fill the rest of the day with interests, hobbies, and relationships. Don't forget animals and plants. You'll have a lot to include in a day.

Let's say the character has a job interview on Wednesday— fill that in. Then backtrack to Monday and make a hair appointment and get your suit cleaned, etc. The calendar provides reality for the life of the character and uncovers what your character is like 24 hours a day, not just during the time of the script. You will have a lot of information, which you have embodied, to bring to the script.

Character Calendar

Monday		Tuesday		Wednesday	

Thursday		Friday		Saturday		Sunday	

Delving into the Character's Psyche and Personality

The Master Switch

L esson 5 introduced working with the character's psyche. When your psyche has been transformed into your character's psyche, your thoughts include the character's issues and thoughts. Your emotional range and depth of emotion will expand beyond your usual emotional boundaries; the actions you take will extend into actions you don't normally take. This work truly reprograms you. If you use your psyche, you have *you*. Reconfiguring your psyche to that of the character, you have the *character*. The following exercise helps you reconfigure your psyche to that of the character. Think of your psyche as a computer program which you will replace with another program.

Exercise to Transform into the Character's Psyche

Do the Preconditioning Exercise (on page 29) and allow your creative self to come foreground.

Answer the following questions to help you distinguish the differences between you (the actor) and your character. To do this look at how you and the character differ in the way you handle life.

- What are my habits? What are the character's habits?
- What are my sensibilities? What are the character's sensibilities?

- What is my occupation? What is the character's occupation?
- What relationships do I have in my life? What relationships does the character have in his life?
- What is my personality like? What is the character's personality like?
- Locate your own thought mechanism. Is it logical and ordered? Is it creative? Is it telegraphic?
- Locate your character's mental activity—the mechanics of his thought. How does he think?

Talking about the following things, speak about them in a soft voice, as you embody what you are saying into your own psyche. Allow the character's psyche to saturate yours until you feel a shift in your own psyche, physical life, emotional life or mood.

- Are the character's thoughts deeper, darker, more brooding or lighter than mine?
- Is the character more anxious or less than I am?
- Is the character more trusting or less than I am?
- Does the character feel more or less separate than I do?
- Is the character more or less yielding?
- More available or less so?
- More or less alienated than I am?
- What's at my character's center?
- What motivates my character?
- What is my character's major issue?
- What is my character's major concern?
- Name another concern.
- What is my character's temperament like? Is he

explosive, moody, temperamental, stormy, shy, hesitant, risky?
- What satisfies this character's psyche?

What kind of body has grown out of my character's psyche? Is it withdrawn and bent over? Is it straight, fluid, and flexible? Is the body fleshy, sensual, angular, quick, ready? Feel the difference in your body.

Get a sense of how things are altering for you. You might need to shift your body. As you do this exercise you will notice you are wanting to hold your body differently; there may be a new expression on your face; you might feel physiological changes such as your heartbeat and body warmth.

- What else has the psyche managed?
- Has it given me a lot of style?
- Do I have mannerisms that bring others to me? Or, mannerisms that keep people away—that intimidate people?
- Do others admire me? What in my character's body and inner being draws people to me in admiration?
- How does the physical body align with my thinking? Do I metabolize quickly? Am I angular with a quick rhythm? Am I muscular?
- Do I take care of myself and others? Am I frail and put together in a way that draws others to help me?

Remember, when your body is transformed into a character it helps you take new kinds of actions. PERSONALITY IS THE OUTER MANIFESTATION OF THE INNER PSYCHE. It is our socialized self; it is how we make our way in the world and how we win. The choice of an occupation is motivated by the psyche.

Our personality forms to satisfy the needs of the psyche as well as to make us competent at the things we need and want, including our occupation.

Allow the information you learned from this exercise to work on you. Continue to program the character's psyche into your own. But, when you're at rehearsal, keep your attention on the interplay between you and those you are working with. Stay close to your impulses and play ball. Never try to do an exercise or hold onto it while you're rehearsing or performing. Let your impulses lead and respond naturally. Just as the psyche (the master switch) filters and guides your emotions, you have the ability to program your psyche to be the character's psyche. Simply said, you set it up and then you hand it over to the psyche.

Mark Kassen says, "Sande's approach is that you kind of program yourself like a computer, working up your character. Then when it's time to go, you do something very simple where you center yourself, you tune into yourself, and then just let it fly."

Behavior

"Follow the life, not the words, and the words will fall into place."

A n actor's job is to create behavior, not words. The words will become rich and alive when they are the result, not the cause, of what is occurring. Behavior cannot be repeated. It comes from natural responses to stimuli—whether the stimulus originates from inside of you or comes from an outside source. The actor has to listen and allow the natural response to these impulses. It is just as important to work this way for theater as it is for the camera.

If you plan your behavior, that is, preplan where you smile, laugh or wink, you risk mugging. Preplanning inhibits your impulse response system. Setting your response stops your creative energy and natural responses.

Obviously, you have an obligation and a commitment to follow your marks and to fulfill the blocking and staging, as well as the demands of the script. If another character says, "Thanks for the coffee," then you must have given him coffee. But, experiencing your actions affects you emotionally in a different way from one performance to another; from one take to another. If you freeze your behavior, it locks in the rest.

Actors search for spontaneity and spontaneity lives in the world of behavior. Think of a film you recently saw and liked? Do you remember more of the words or the interesting behavior?

Behavioral Mode

Your psyche shows itself in your behavior. You behave by living in the condition that you have created. The life of the MOMENT is happening before you speak. If you turn on the television without the sound, you know who the characters are before you can hear their voices. Likewise, if you see a person on the street who seems dangerous, you can usually intuit the threat by their behavioral mode. You can read a person leaning against a wall or standing and thinking or entering a room, before any accompanying action or activity occurs.

Exercise on Behavior

Note: When you do this exercise, allow it to come to you. Give yourself time to embellish upon everything you say. Challenge yourself by questioning, "What else can I say about that?"

1. Do the Preconditioning Exercise on page 29 and allow your creative self to come to the foreground.

2. Each person or character has a system of behavior. Beginning with yourself, discuss your own mode of behavior. Are you temperamental or quick to respond in a defensive way? Are you aloof and standoffish? Are you laid-back and easygoing? And so on.

3. Now begin to speak about your character's temperament and behavior. Include it into the already formed condition (see Condition Exercise on page 105). This behavior will be visible to an audience before any action or spoken word.

Behavioral Action

A behavioral action is one that *can* be planned and repeated. This is an action that can annoy or distract or emphasize. Behavioral action is a repeatable action, trait, activity or gesture needed to fulfill a required action in the script or is one of your intuitive choices.

Perhaps your character is required to throw over a table. Three lines before that action, the character could begin swinging a leg, which results in the table being thrown over.

Sitting

The way Al Pacino sits, as any of his characters, inspired this exercise. There is always a very visceral, powerful energy in how he sits, which seems to be informed by his character. Don't confuse this exercise with trying to find out how your character sits. This exercise is about the point of power coming from the way you sit. It is a sitting "psychology," and provides a strong connecting link between you and the character.

Sitting Exercise

Sit in a chair and allow your energy to go down into your backside. Let all of the circumstances and your knowledge of the character's personality and energy become embodied in the way you sit. Shift around a little bit until you get into the sense or "groove" of the character. Eventually, allow the energy to move up and distribute throughout the body.

Attributes

Here is an exercise for transforming your energy into that of the character's.

It's worth saying again and again that transformation into character always begins with yourself—your own body, psyche, emotional body, sensitivities, vulnerabilities, and so on.

Attributes are a specific property inherent to each person. For our use, there is a wrapping together, an entwining, of a few different elements of the character. When you do this, you create a new system of energy—a palpable energetic, a new physicality, a new approach. Working with attributes is a very direct way of creating an entirely new system for the character; after which you can discover the role.

Exercise on Attributes

1. Do the Preconditioning Exercise on page 29 and allow your creative self to come to the foreground.

2. With your eyes still closed, choose a character attribute: deeply lonely, highly inquisitive, intelligent, piercing fiery rhythm, cool or detached.

3. Speak about one of your character's attributes: " 'Highly visible' brings out the best in me, it makes me charming, I stand straight, my head is held high, I am aware of my far head and jaw."

4. Look through your body and determine where this attribute is located within you. Observe what it does to your body. " 'Highly visible,' for me, is in my jaw. It makes my head pull back while my jaw juts forward."

5. What does this attribute do to your energy? " 'Highly visible' excites me, it puts me on go, pushes me forward."

6. What does this attribute do to your approach? " 'Highly visible' makes me focused, gathers energy to my center, makes me acutely conscious of what is going on around me."

Work with two additional attributes and repeat steps 2 through 6. This works best when you choose two of your character's attributes that are in contrast to one another. Then you will feel pushed and pulled in different directions physically and energetically. When working the third attribute, notice what happens to your energy system as you have three different attributes working at once.

This exercise will help you to set up a new energy system, nervous response system, physicality and approach which will trigger a new action pattern for your character. It will lead you to a new approach to the character and new actions, while using the words from the script.

Central Thrust

I call central thrust the context for the character's motivation; It is at the character's center. It influences how he is and how he behaves. Central thrust is nothing that is strived for. It is not an action. It is a way of being, from which the character creates his world. The character is motivated through his central thrust, as well as through the circumstances in his life.

Central thrust provides the actor with the character's behavior, actions and motivation. Look at how the character puts central thrust in place with the example of control. Control can be carried out by dominating others, being very charming, or being excellent at what you do. Possibilities of central thrust, other than control, might include intimacy, power, success, romance, and so on.

Let's look at a character who has a control issue at his center. The set-up is that he is having a fight with his partner. She is yelling at him while he stands there cutting very thin slices of cheese exactly the same size and shape and then tasting it. All the while, his partner is getting more and more upset by the way he is responding. Good action, right?

Central thrust . . . . .control
Motivation . . . . .upsetting partner
Activity . . . . .slicing cheese

Exercise on Central Thrust

1. Do the Preconditioning Exercise (on page 29) and bring your creative self to the foreground.

2. Using yourself as an example, explore what's at your center and how it shows up in your life.

3. Now switch and work with your character:
   • What's at my character's center and how does it show up behaviorally and in the actions he takes during each scene?
   • What key lines in the material indicate the central thrust?
   • What are my character's actions?
   • What are my character's qualities?

Lifestyles Diary

For me, one of the most exciting aspects of acting is being able to experience another person's lifestyle. The following exercise enables you to do that.

1. Ask yourself "What do I have to *set up* to experience the character's lifestyle?"

2. Create a diary for your character.

3. Maybe your character is very wealthy and you don't have the experience of what it's like to be wealthy. Set up and participate in an event, such as a shopping trip to Barney's or Rodeo Drive, tea at the Plaza Hotel in New York City, or a few hours at a country club. This will help you sense how the character's life and priorities are different from your own.

4. Then ask, "What do I have to change in myself to be able to live that lifestyle?" Keep recording in the diary. What do you have to change in yourself, and what do you notice is changing because of the exercise. After a while, you might actually find yourself notating thoughts that the character is informing you about.

5. Compiling the date book (refer to page 85) is a quiet exercise done alone and helps you to penetrate your character's life more deeply using your imagination and intuition. The lifestyles diary gives you the experience of aspects of a character's life that you're not familiar with.

It is more of an event and involves a certain amount of research.

Buying a Newspaper

An Active Exercise

This is a simple exercise. Go out and buy a newspaper as your character. Be very attentive while dressing to what your character might be wearing. Be in touch with your impulses. Where do you, as the character, put your keys? Do you wear a hat or not? Where do you keep your money?

Leave your house with the character's issues, not yours, on your mind. While walking to the newspaper stand, try to solve an issue in the character's life. When you reach the newsstand, which newspaper or magazine calls your attention? You can use this exercise any time you run errands. Note: I would not do this for serious shopping, as the character will inform you. I was working closely with Chris Gillis while he was choreographing his first dance piece for the Paul Taylor Dance Company. On the way to rehearsal and thinking about some possibilities for the piece, I passed a store in SoHo that was featuring a little white net tutu-type skirt. It was so unlike anything I would wear, even in my dreams, but I was drawn to it and bought it. After rehearsal the energy of dance wore off and I looked at my purchase with my usual taste. With a laugh, I learned the lesson of how we are informed by the character. (I say, once again, allow the character to inform you but not while you are shopping for yourself.)

Taking a Shower Exercise

Take a two-minute shower as yourself. Be aware of how you take a shower. Do you have music playing? Do you sing or stretch? What are you thinking about?

Now, create your bathroom as best you can into one your character might be using. Let your impulses guide you. Would your character listen to music? Is her rhythm and taste in music different from yours? What does the character think about in the shower? What concerns and issues are at the forefront in the character's mind? You will probably have a lot of differences between yourself and the character that you can incorporate into the role.

PART FOUR

Rehearsal

Rehearsal

The work you've done for homework is with you on a cellular level; don't try to hold on to it when you work with others. Stay in relationship, contact, communicate, land and make an impact. Make your partner brilliant. There is no room for blaming a nonresponsive partner. Get in his face and make him great. Make him respond. If you are upset, use it to shake him up. Keep your listening open and be receptive. All of your behavior and impulses depend upon your listening. Transforming into your character is building new muscle, which you have already begun. Rehearsing, which you are now up to, is playing ball. Rehearsal is the time for you to emerge from all of the work that you have done alone and to test it out. You will find yourself discarding some things and keeping and adding others. Now is your chance to work with (and off) other actors. Projects are built on strong community.

"Let the theatricality come out of the quiet.
Go deeply into your center. Your power
will come out of the silence."

So far, you have looked at your script with a new perception and looked at yourself with a new image in mind. Hopefully, you have worked some of the on-paper exercises and have done some of the more active ones. You are different. You'll be drawn to new things. Perhaps you will find yourself attracted to antiques instead of modern furniture for the first time in your life. You might find you are sitting on a shorter fuse both temperamentally and psychologically. Your responses and your appearance are not the same.

Go to your rehearsals ready for action, for communication, for interplay with others. When you rehearse, you need to work on a new focus (layering). Each new focus will take you more deeply into the underlying dynamics of the material, the complexities of the relationship and the vividness of the moment.

Opening Moments

The following exercises will bring you to a heightened, exciting, connected opening moment. Your entrance will be steeped in an already established condition, including an emotional state that is comprised of what you are presently going through and where you are coming from.

Whether you are speaking or not, the audience must be able to read what is going on for you. What you say comes out of your emotional state. As you work on these exercises, use a tape recorder, a partner, or an eyes closed technique. (Open your eyes only to read the next instruction.)

Condition into Emotional State

Condition is an established emotional and psychological state (an inner climate) that informs where you are coming from. Everything comes out of that Condition—words, actions, emotional response. Condition allows the actor to have many different things happening at one time; it includes point of view, intention, mood, logistical (running up stairs) and sensorial (sweating, or just being wet) data. Condition could include the character's focus on specific issues and concerns as he enters the scene.

To create Condition, start with the sense of being an empty vessel that becomes filled. Use the next exercise to help you experience Condition.

Exercise on Condition

1. Discuss the place, the mood, and the atmosphere.

2. What is the character's intention? Add pertinent circumstances and operative facts.

3. Discuss and elaborate on the logistical and sensorial data, beginning with one minute before the actual scene. Use data like, "I've been caught in traffic," "I'm running up five flights of stairs," "I just woke up," "It's cold," "It's hot," "I'm hungry." Where, specifically, is the character coming from? Might it be the theater or a date, etc.? What effect does this time before have on YOU? What are you physically carrying? Have you gone shopping? Do you have

groceries or a new dress? All of this will affect your mood and what you actually do when you enter a new scene.

4. Review the character's issue in the scene. This issue, plus the mood created by step 3, will create the condition with which you will approach your opening moment.

5. What is your emotional state related to? If, For example, your opening moment is answering the door to let your date in, you might choose to be involved in the hassle or excitement of dressing or having concerns about how the date may go. Then, as you answer the door, let the new moment move in on you and take it from there. Be creative with what you choose. Try different choices at rehearsal and see the state it puts you into for an opening moment.

6. Do this exercise on the way to rehearsal.

Everyone comes from some place, and that needs to be expressed in behavior, mood, emotional tone, action, and relationship, as well as the verbal expression.

State

State is a combination of mood, feelings and thoughts that puts you into a specific emotional condition, such as distraught, distracted, amused, etc. Condition also includes how other incidents such as weather, food, alcohol, affect you, what just happened to you and how you feel about all of it.

State is created by:

- The physical (posture, facial expressions: smiling, frowning, etc.)
- The physiological (running, thoughts, etc.)
- The verbal (talking about what excites or depresses you)
- Music and other sound
- Visual: paintings, pictures, art
- Taking an action (slamming a door)

State is a grand prize in that, unlike emotions, it can be created and repeated. Since you can actually generate state, use it often.

The word "state" also relates to how you want to be seen. It is the socialization of real feelings. The primary aspect of working the state is, always feel what you are really feeling and then put the state on top of that. Just as in life, say, you are going to work and not feeling very well. Your boss, someone you see only occasionally, walks into the room and says, "How are you?" You probably would not say, "Oh, I feel awful." We usually are a little more socialized than that; unless your particular job situation and relationship with your boss warrants it. The same concept applies to acting. In rehearsal and working on a scene, you find yourself wanting to slap your partner and run out of the room. Okay, that's what is really going on for you in the scene. But, your director wants you to walk towards the other actor and embrace him. Yes, he really means it. He wants you to put your arms around the actor that you now dislike intensely. What do you do? You simply use your thoughts to justify the state, which might be, "I'll never let him see me this angry." Now you have created a state of how you want him to see you, combined with your real feelings. So you and the director both win.

Real feelings usually begin to align with the state. Allow the circumstances and Psyche to feed you. If your feelings don't automatically respond that way, allow the Psyche to feed you with more interior monologue. Soon enough a cut-together between you and the character will come into play. You will know when it happens. It's like being in action and very silent at the same time.

As you work with state, refer back to Lesson 7 on "Interior Monologue" and to Part Three on "Circumstances and Operative Facts." In addition, use the emotional body, allowing the emotions to flow freely, so that what you're feeling will convert in response to well-embodied circumstances and operative facts. Remember, the circumstances, as with every aspect of this technique, have to be relevant, meaningful and true for you, for the character, and to the emotional tone of the scene.

Choices

"Choices are to an actor as a stethoscope is to a doctor."

As people and as actors, we are always making choices. Choices arise as soon as we turn our attention outward from the inner psyche. Choices are emotional. A child sees a cookie and eats the cookie. He says "Cookie!" and eats it. Whereas adults see a cookie, make the choice that they want it, and then the mental process of decision enters. "Should I eat the cookie? If I have a cookie, it really ought to be the best cookie," and on and on. We need to stay close to our natural responses and feelings when making choices.

Ask yourself some of these questions to help you embody choices:

- What is the choice about?
- Where do I want it to go?
- What is the intention behind the choice?
- What do I need to know about the scene?
- What do I want the specific rehearsal or perform-ance to be about?

Make choices about relationship, place and your point of view. Don't manipulate your emotions, but get a sense of how you feel toward the other characters. The circumstances as well as stylis-tic and cultural factors will help you to make great choices.

Trust your impulses! Trust your first choice! When you're in a parked car you don't go anywhere. When you're driving you might veer a bit to the left or a bit to the right, but being in mo-tion helps you to make corrections and stay on the path. You do not have to be right. Just stay in action!

Exercise on Choices

Focus on choices your character could make:

- Do I want the scene to be more suspenseful?

- Do I want my character to feel threatened or tense
  or in some sort of danger?

If it doesn't move you, make another choice. You must make a choice that stirs you, one you can live into. If you are going to wear a red dress or shirt, be ready to be looked at. In other words, make your choices as bold as possible and stay in the moment with them. Choices keep you in the moment. They keep things new and prevent you from trying to do yesterday's work.

While working with an actor on a scene in *Closer,* we used choices as a way to get him to open up to his character. He felt that the character was weak and not very attractive. He didn't like him and certainly did not want to transform himself into this character. I suggested that a strong choice would be for him to go to the doctor's office and if necessary have a physical fight with the doctor. He was to get the doctor to give him the girl they both desired.

It didn't matter whether the action was written into the script. He had to look for the moment to fight for the girl. It didn't matter that the fight never occurs. This choice gave the actor something to work for and he was able to see another side to his character.

Tone

Tone guides the emotional orchestration of the material, as it guides and directs the emotional intensity. It is similar to the relationship between a conductor and the musicians in an orchestra. When we look at a scene and peg it as "angry," there is nowhere else to go. We feel obligated to be angry. Instead, if we interpret the tone as confrontational, argumentative, and tumultuous, there is room for fear, hesitancy, or explosiveness and even humor, as well as anger. How many times have we become aware of ourselves in the midst of an argument and felt silly or rather ridiculous for being so upset over practically nothing?

Become aware of the tone in the rooms that you enter this week. It will make you sensitive to the tone that you are reading about in the script. What are your responses to those tones? What do they make you want to do?

Tone Exercise

Draw or chart a graph of the ups and downs, the pitch, the emotional volatility, or subtlety of a scene. Allow it to guide your intensity without dictating a specific emotion. It makes you rise to the sound of the material.

Thru-Line and Main Action

Your thru-line is the journey through the show. Your main action is the act of fulfillment that helps you achieve the thru-line. To see the character's thru-line (journey), we look at the whole body of material: how he travels or lives his life in the entire play. Through it, we see how he is different from the beginning to the end. We see his main action, how he attains his goals and fulfills his overall objective. If the character's thru-line is to get ready to perform, the main action might be to feel good about yourself, to get you ready for a performance.

If Blanche's thru-line, in *A Streetcar Named Desire,* is to hold on to her fantasies, her main action would be to make up fantastic stories about her past.

For the character Austin, in Sam Shepard's play *True West,* if his thru-line is to deal with the distractions of his brother, his main action could be to finish the script and achieve his objective of getting his movie made.

In your life, it is amazing when you look beyond its incidents and recognize a thru-line to it. You see just how purposeful your life really is.

Intention

"We learn in particles, intention organizes them."

Intention sets everything in motion for life and for one's character. All of your inner potential has the possibility of becoming a project through intention. Similarly your character's life is set in motion intentionally. His intention motivates fulfilling his goals, the scene objective and his main action. As we do with every aspect of this technique, choose an intention that personally stirs you. Intention is the force that keeps the actor out in the field.

Your intentions fuel your actions, and whether you like the results or not, intention is always working.

The Action

"Response lives in the moment."

T he action is what you do to someone. Pick an action, a response, from what is being done to you. If you are being aggressed upon or seduced or laughed at, what does that make you feel? What does it provoke in you? What action can you take? Word the action in a way that is relevant for you. You have an opportunity to express yourself through the action in a way that you might not have in your own life. Take the action of "getting you away from me." How many people would you like to "get away from you"? You see what I mean? This gives the scene a resounding, truthful experience.

In *A Streetcar Named Desire*, Blanche, feeling threatened by Stanley's aggressive behavior, might take the action of avoiding him, pushing him away from her or putting him down.

If someone bumps you in the street you know what action to take. It is not a cerebral, it's an emotional reaction.

Relationship

"Judging eats up passion."

R elationship takes relatedness—being related to all things, the people, the place, and all of the elements involved in the scene. As with life, the further out you go with relationship, the more memorable moments you will have, the more you push the envelope, the more exciting things are. Relationship, at its best, takes place outside of you. Look first at the more obvious relationships such as mother and daughter, husband and wife, doctor and patient, director and actor. Explore the relatedness under the formality of the relationship; look at the humanity involved and the human feelings of two or more people. Knowing that someone is your boyfriend or girlfriend does little good unless you know how you feel about them.

All of your thoughts, considerations and judgments are inside. When you allow a relationship to take you beyond your comfort zone and predisposition, you have the possibility of a relationship beyond your limitations, thus outside of you. Then whenever you need an anchor, go back to relationship and connect. Contact, communicate, land and be open to the other.

To take relationship outside of yourself, think of this very moment in a relationship as being a crossroads:

- Where you step into a new way of being together;
- Where you search for what is new rather than having it as you know it to be;
- Where you break an energy cycle or recurring behavior;
- Whenever you break a pattern and take a different approach, relationship can give you a new opportunity to go beyond yourself;
- Make your partner brilliant, get in their face and wake them up.

Relationship is a primary tool for rehearsal.

Exercise on Relationship

Establish your point of view about your character's relationship with another and address the following issues:

- What is your character's major issue or concern about this relationship?
- What is possible at the crossroads in this relationship? Let the give-and-take of this relationship and the moment alter the crossroads.
- What is at stake in this relationship?
- How does the relationship change from beginning to end?
- Always keep your own feelings for the other person alive. You can only work with your own true feelings; there are no feelings but your own.

Turning Points

"We reinvent ourselves daily."

I mention turning points again now, as they are a way of creating more changes as you are rehearsing. Turning points, covered in Lesson 8, are a great focus for layering because turning points create change. They orchestrate the material, keep the tension between actors, and make a valuable focus for rehearsal. A turning point occurs whenever you discover change, have a conflict, win or lose, or have a new understanding.

Something is new—different than it was before. The difference
might be in the character's status, situation or relationship—a
change of tone, mood and emotional impact. There is a change
in the way you are. You take different actions because of the
turning points, and the approaches and the tone are different.
At every turning point a new octave is reached and the en-
gagement and intensity escalate. At the moment of change the
level of energy, relatedness, and at-stake-ness all spiral up to a
new octave. Don't let the ball drop. The tension must remain
between actors even if one actor has all the words and the other
is just listening.

In Sam Shepard's play *True West,* Hollywood producer (Sol)
buys Lee's idea for a movie and drops the option for Austin's
movie (Lee's brother); here is a very dramatic turning point.
There is a role reversal: Austin takes on the behavior and identity of his brother Lee.

Beats

Break the script into beats after you work with the other actors and have feedback from the director. A beat is a
change of objective. It is usually thought of as a change of action, but that is not necessarily true, because you can change
your action many times while still going for the same objective.

If my objective is to get a play produced, I can take the following actions; the actions change but the objective remains
the same.

- Present readings of the material to an invited audience;
- Make phone calls to producers and investors;
- Do mailings;
- Take an ad in newspapers and journals;
- Direct a showcase.

Make a list for yourself of ten actions you can take, with just one specific person to get them interested in producing your project.

To find the beats, trace the action. When the action changes continue to read on; does what you are going for seem to have changed? At the end of a beat you usually win, lose or draw.

You can feel a completion for that moment.

Turning points and beats are related in that they both result in change; they differ in that within a beat there may be many turning points.

Impulses and Interruptions

Impulses are ongoing. They don't come on cue. When you hear a word or idea that stimulates or calls up any response at all, begin to respond before your cue. Don't actually interrupt verbally, but engage your impulse to interrupt. For example if I say, "The weather outside is..." and you immediately want to respond with something you feel about the weather, such as how cold it is outside or how warm you are, you can respond without the actual words. To understand this point, observe how you automatically want to interrupt others during conversations in your life, whether you actually do so or not.

Creativity

"Think of your projects as your potential, rather than as a goal. The projects come from inside you and move outward as they grow."

Creativity is seeing what can be and is possible, rather than what is and has to be. It is the last topic for this chapter on rehearsal because it is the thread that takes you from inception to rehearsal through performance. Once you begin to rehearse and then to perform, you add the pressures of production, which you have to be able to work WITH, but not be consumed BY. Creativity is your key.

To be creative, we wait for inspiration; actually it is when we are creative that we are inspired.

Focusing on doing things right, or trying to figure out what THEY want, is antithetical to the development of creativity. Be who you are and let them see YOU. Be great, be bold, be creative. (When you go to an audition, do the same thing—be who you are—show up—and let THEM see YOU. You will either be what they are looking for or not. If you are not, and you are memorable, you may very well be called in for the next project.)

Throw your creativity out in front of you and let it inspire you to greatness. This means living and working outside the dictates of time, space, and your own mental limitations, which we all have.s

Example: You might think it has to take a certain amount of time to develop a good relationship, but that same relationship can happen instantly. You might think the same way about a script that you are working on. However, if you are open to it, and expect it, it can come to you very quickly. Take a chance and go beyond who you are at the present time. There is always more of you than you realize.

When you feel pressured, or even if you don't and just want the optimum conditions for your work, keep reaching for your creativity.

To work in the spirit of creativity, rehearse one of the scenes from the script fulfilling the dynamics of the scene rather than the scene itself. Rehearse in a style that is evoked by the underlying dynamics. The style might be a dream, a nightmare, children at play, a western, an opera, an action movie, seduction, a ballet, a thriller, a nursery rhyme, or a grade B movie. Take what you have found about the character or the material from this open and creative rehearsal and bring it to the script itself.

PART FIVE

Auditioning and Private Coaching

Being Prepared for Your Auditions

D o not try to get ready at the last minute. Live in a state of readiness. Make readiness your way of life. When you are in gear, then you can focus on each audition fully and not suddenly have to be at 100 percent in energy, attention, and being present. You are already there! I should say, you're already here! This readiness circumvents last-minute scrambles for clothes, accessories, pictures and résumés, and material (if a monologue is required). You will know what to wear for the kind of roles you are auditioning for. You should find an acting school where you can learn and which you can utilize as a gym to keep yourself tuned. When you are ready, private coaching will assist you in being the best you can be for your audition or performance.

Private Coaching

In my opinion, you will always show up better for auditions and in performance when you are privately coached. Private coaching is the fine-tuning that can usually come only from a trained outside eye looking in. It is expensive, so the actor should weigh and evaluate the importance of the project against the expense of the coaching. Private coaching can be as vital for a seasoned actor as it is for a newcomer. Choose a coach who is not only extremely talented at his or her craft but one with whom you personally resonate.

I love to private coach. It affords me a closeup of when an actor finds the connecting links into character; the "route in" varies with each actor. I cried throughout the last day of coaching Matthew Modine into the role of Dave for the TV movie remake of *Flowers for Algernon*. Not only did the script touch me deeply but the experience of where Matthew was going and what he himself felt once he connected into the role, was what brought me to tears. I watched as he found his way into the role physically, working with a great deal of imagination and courage.

While coaching Ginger Prince for the role of M'Lynn in the original New York Off-Broadway cast of *Steel Magnolias*, I knew the moment kicked in when she began moving her arms up and down the arms of the chair as she watched over the last minutes of her daughter's life.

Coaching Michelle Hicks for her first film role of Penny in *Twin Falls, Idaho*, we stayed low to the ground. We did that intuitively to keep an easy tone to the room. The film itself felt very low to the ground to me, as many scenes took place in chairs and beds. At one point I asked Michelle to slide down a wall. She asked, "How? Where will I find a wall? It takes place in the street." I suggested she find a building or street light. It worked beautifully in the film.

I coached Mark Kassen by telephone for his role in TV's *Third Watch.* For the Off-Broadway show, *Things You Shouldn't Say Past Midnight,* Mark, by using his own current life, connected to one of the lines of the script ("I am everywhere"). He spilled his heart out and got to the truth, the deep undeniable truth, of where he is right now in his life and gave it to his character.

Anthony Rapp genuinely grasps the essence, spirit and behavior of a character, and is very savvy about knowing what has to happen in a scene. Going in just with that, he gets the inner connection.

These are some examples of actors making inner connections from the physical of Matthew to the emotional of Ginger to the personal references of Mark and the artistic abstractions of Anthony. Each actor works differently. How they work and when and where they connect is personal—the point is they all do connect.

A good coach will help you find the path best for you and your instrument and will help you know the nature of the material. Look inside of you! Everything is within you. Each script will siphon up usable elements from inside you for you to use for the character.

We are in a privileged position as performers. Audiences see themselves through us: new prototypes, new possibility, new answers to life's dynamic questions.

What we need as performers, to be able to accomplish this, is the same as we need as human beings—to consistently design life anew.

Experiences of Private Coaching

Michelle Hicks

During a private with Sande, I realized that at auditions, I was being paced by the person I was reading with. Although I had the character, knew what was going on in the scene, and really went there emotionally during my sessions with Sande, at auditions, my performance would be based on who I was reading with.

One of my biggest assets as an actress is my ability to be in relationship and to create with and work off of another actor. Now I'm learning how to come in with my performance no matter who I'm reading with for an audition, or who I'm cast with for a film.

Shalome Harlow

While working with Sande I defined my role in my first film *In and Out* and began working on the emotional aspects of the character. First I connected to myself, to my own emotions, that is, feeling what I was truly feeling. I was aware of the sensations going through me and that these sensations connected me to my character and my own emotional body. I would breathe deeply and allow myself to connect to a silent space within, before saying the words.

When my emotional body is available, I can work with my intention and main action and still have the capability to express spontaneously and to feel new in each take.

Brandi Burkhardt

I came to Sande after my year as Miss New York. I had been out of class for a year and had lost my inspiration to act. Sande changed all of that. I found, through working privately and in her intensive, and later in regular class, that Sande's technique far surpassed any I had studied. I saw immediate results in my work. It is difficult to understand if you have not experienced her technique yourself, but she gives you the tools to be completely comfortable and real, and not to be self-conscious. By looking at the script as a road map you allow the "Character's Story" to emerge from the script, and through investigating the similarities and differences you have with the character, you are able to create what becomes known as "Your Story" as the character. The secret is, you never turn yourself off. I used to wonder where a character's life begins and where the actor's life ends, but it doesn't work that way at all. The character's life begins before the play begins and the actor's life never ends. You enhance the character. It is a reprogramming of sorts.

Not only has this taught me about being a better actor, but also it has taught me to be a better person

"We all recognize greatness. It takes us out of ourselves and lifts us to the best we can be."

Broadway's Hero's

Eight shows a week!
If a drama, one turns oneself inside out facing one's truths,

one's demons, and being vulnerable under any and all conditions.

For Broadway musicals, the actor might be doing some or all of the above, as well as tap dancing on rooftops, sliding down scaffolding, singing fifteen songs and saying I love you while projecting to the balcony.

What is needed, you ask?

- Commitment
- Talent
- Perseverance
- Presence
- Going 100 percent every time
- Allowing that something special to shine through

Celebrities of Film

Action! Cut! Print!

On the set at 7 A.M. or earlier, makeup for hours, sitting in your trailer between takes, jumping through the hoop 20 times and each time with a new twist. Then reaching in and pulling it all up, looking for the truth, staying true to what you're feeling, feeling all that the script siphons up in you, staying ready for 12 hours and then the big scene shoots just when you thought you'd leave for your kid's birthday celebration.

What is needed, you ask?

- Commitment
- Talent
- Perseverance
- Presence

- Going 100 percent every time
- Allowing that something special to shine through

TV Stars

The power of the media!

No thought going unseen by the camera; millions of people watching at one time, we depend on all of the quality programming and news shows to bring life once beyond our homes, into our everyday reality.

There are so many to acknowledge who make a significant day to day impact on our lives. To name a few: Barbara Walters, The View, HBO for their quality and inventive programming, CNN for their exceptional news coverage, Larry King, and then there are entertainment shows like West Wing that bring difficult subject matter to new and informative levels. Hosts like Oprah and Rosie share their lives, tragedies, failures, wins, strengths, weaknesses and wisdom for the good of humanity.

What is needed, you ask?

- Commitment
- Talent
- Perseverance
- Presence
- Going 100 percent every time
- Allowing that something special to shine through

They all do whatever is needed. Will You?

PART SIX

Performance

Performance

"People say, 'If God wanted us to fly, we would have been given wings.' We were. She gave us Performance."

I spent my childhood dreaming and my adulthood fulfilling those dreams, through my work as a director, actor, acting teacher and coach. I love brilliance and I applaud any and all techniques that guide the actor to that exuberant state of unlimited creativity called performance. This book has brought you into a new relationship with your creative self; it has taken you through a technique that has been developed for the working actor in all media. How, then, is performance made different because of the work? Some letters I have collected from actors who I work with, give you their first hand experience of performing using this technique. I can tell you that getting to that desired state of letting go, of surrender, of being totally present without judgment or limitation, of being exalted and highly energized yet steady and clear, is a STEP AWAY rather than WORLDS AWAY from your normal state.

Performance is a mystical experience and everyone has to find their own way to get there. It is not an ordinary way of being. It takes the ability to surrender, to focus and to take action, just as an athlete does. Everything you encounter on the way, you can surmount with strong commitment.

Find your own way. With nerves being one of the biggest challenges; breathe, don't try to ignore them. Work with the interior monologue exercise on page 57. Complete your nervous thought with that of the character's. Focus on your breath and in getting into the groove of the character and the performing zone.

A time comes when the work is done and your spirit guides you. What gets you from here (ordinary reality) to there (performance reality), is moving up into the zone; call it go, call it action, call it readiness, it's time for performance.

Performance Experiences by My Students

Tripp Hanson

The latest in a series of show business adventures has me on Broadway in a capacity which I could never have imagined—I'm covering six different roles in a Broadway musical! Yeow!!!

It's one thing to get hired to play a specific character and go through the luxury of the rehearsal process with all of the other actors and the director and choreographer—things happen in relationship to the others and as a result of direction, etc, etc, etc.

All of this makes great sense to me, and to this I know how to apply technique!

It's another thing to be hired after the rehearsal process was over and the show was already in previews. In fact the director would be leaving within the week . . .

Six roles!

Hmmm.

Flash forward...few weeks later:

"Tripp, please report to the stage manager's office."

I hadn't even gotten half way down the stairs when other cast members on their way up clued me in..."I think you're on for Blake...he's not feeling so good..."

My mind starts racing...I've never even rehearsed the big number that opens Act 2, the one he's featured in. I've never done the scene immediately after—or the quick change in between—but it's not that hard, right? OK...I can do this!

Meanwhile, Blake's dressers are coming towards me with directives about how this change will happen, and where to meet them for that change... "The wig will be on the landing." "Does he have a mustache for the finale?" "Get him to the costume department to take Blake's costume in for him . . ."

"Five minutes, ladies and gentlemen."

Now the dance captain is standing with me at my dressing table, people are trying to pin costumes on me, handing me props that I've never held before in my life!

"Do you know your pattern for the end of 'Too Darn Hot'? Are you good with 'the floyd' (a flurry of steps created by Kathleen Marshall, the brilliant choreographer of the show on the day that hurricane Floyd hit New York, and so named in its honor!!).

"I think so..." My heart is in my throat at this point. Technique?!

"Places, ladies and gentlemen...places for Act 2."

I can't focus. I'm going to die! The shock takes hold.

And there I am. Onstage, in front of a full house on Broadway—underrehearsed, hardly prepared, and feeling as if at any moment I might leave my body.

The number takes place in the alley outside a theater in Baltimore on a dead hot summer night. The cast is looking for a breath of fresh air, and—as it must in musical theater—a huge dance number ensues! It starts out with a slow tattoo drummed on a crate ... by whom? Who else! I have to start this number. I'm having trouble even breathing yet, I have to set the tempo from whence the rest of this number will progress!

Technique. I do have a point. It took hold of me. I know what my moment is ... I know how to begin, by opening my listening. I know this character, this situation—the revelry of a company of players, looking for ways to amuse and entertain each other in the midst of the disaster occurring between our stars ...

Hey! I know this. I hear Sande say, "Tripp, surrender ... the circumstances will carry you."

Of course I'm nervous and I argue with myself (and with the Sande in my head!), "Yeah, but will they carry me on the right beat and the right foot?!"

"Just breathe, Tripp ... fall in."

But wait! All of this emotion. This is the emotional body in its finest form. Raw energy waiting to be shaped by the events at hand, by the relationships.

I've been studying at Sande's studio for 19 years. It is in me, in my psyche. I've taught the technique for the last nine of these years. And now, at this moment which feels a lot like "crisis management," is when it feels like the best possible place to let myself just be.

Were there mistakes? Technical errors? Yep. Nothing major, but some details. I survived!

Were there connections made with my fellow actors? You bet! Did those relationships count more than perfection? In my opinion, yes; this is why I've worked with Sande all these years.

Second nature... what technique should be. There, ready to inform any moment. Our job is just to make ourselves available to it. Simple, but, like a motor, driving the whole vehicle... readily marrying inner and outer... not looking to criticize WHAT SHOULD BE, but taking WHAT IS, the raw material of life, the perfect potential in every single moment.

It's all well and good to pay lip service to technique when we've rehearsed to perfection, every gesture articulated, every moment explained. But it's the surprise we must be ready for... the newness, the opportunity in any moment... that's when technique will carry us to new heights.

Or it will save our ass.

Either way... believe me... you want technique! Do yourself a favor and build it!

Ginger Prince

In 1987 I got real lucky. I became a member of the original company of *Steel Magnolias*. There were six actresses cast in the roles and three actresses hired to cover them. I was to cover the roles of M'Lynn, the mother played by Rosemary Prinz, and Truvy, the hairdresser, played by Margo Martindale. Two fabulous actresses, two roles at opposite ends of the sensibility spectrum. One outrageously funny, direct and warm, the other, the "Real Steel Magnolia."

Okay!! Now doing this was a challenge. These roles were so different, where do I begin? If I had not had Sande's technique and training, quite frankly, I would have been lost. Each piece of her technique was invaluable as I began to work on these characters, but I found the most useful was her approach to Interior Monologue.

Many times both of my characters were on stage together and talking to each other and interacting. The problem was not the dialogue but how and why the dialogue was there. I had to separate their minds and begin to create or find these characters in me. I had to discover what they were thinking every moment of the play. Actors can never stop thinking on stage—if they do, they are dead. I had to discover their reasoning, apparatus and thought patterns. I started by asking questions, wondering, musing, uncovering—as the character. A character's reaction to a line or an action comes out of the thought process.

The actor must develop a complete system of reasoning and thought for that particular person which is totally unique and different than any other person. The person I was creating thinks, feels and is thrown into action by natural responses-reactions to what is going on, what I am seeing, what I am hearing, what I am feeling. The fascinating thing was to discover how differently Truvy and M'Lynn responded to the same happening (or stimuli).

When I started finding the character in me, the lines became easier to learn and remember and became so very logical. Of course M'Lynn would say that. Of course Truvy would laugh at that. It was so much easier but I always allowed my spontaneous, in-the-moment, responses to come forward—I gave them room to be there, to surprise me and move me forward . . . to give me new insight and understanding.

Having the privilege of working onstage with so many wonderful actresses was mind-blowing at times. We would find new moments, new connections or maybe just a small shared look that meant so much, but had never occurred before. But a look means nothing unless there is a new understanding or a discovery behind it.

Silently, quietly...a new moment...a treasure...a gift of a long run...and working actors...and a usable, vital technique. This interior monologue is like a needle and thread, that weaves you through the play...moment to moment.

Daphne Rubin-Vega

"Sande Shurin" was Anthony Rapp's resolute and booming reply to my question, "I want to study again. Got any suggestions?"

After *Rent,* I did a film, then dove into music. Now, here I was—tweaking my skills. I encountered a class full of enthusiasm, matched if not topped by Sande's own. We discovered, uncovered and tapped into characters as if in a serious playground. What fun to enjoy falling, being the fool and rejoicing in our own limitations.

The fun of performance comes from being prepared, and then having the wings to let go into the unknown. Because I was working with Robert DeNiro in the movie *Flawless,* I wanted to create a character whose demonstration of love for him was poignant and clear. With Sande's help I created a character that was solidly hooked within me; I then could be open to suggestions, improvements and changes from the director.

For my lead in an indie film, *Skeleton Woman,* Sande and I worked beat by beat, breaking down the progression of the script. I knew what each section was about, how I came into the scene and what I was up to in the scene.

Sande saw my performance in *Gum* and after the show had opened, there we were trying new approaches in two of the scenes.

There is a passion, curiosity and generosity that informs

Sande's work and inspires mine. As a teacher she cuts through the superfluous and guides us to do the same. We create a carefully chosen armature into which we can breathe life through our own truthfulness and spontaneity. Sande, thank you and bless you.

Christianne Tisdale

I am a person who loves and lives for "firsts" . . . first kisses, first encounters, first spoonfuls of Skippy peanut butter. For me, it never gets better. How lucky for me that I've met Sande Shurin.

Being in the moment and working from moment to moment constantly informs and transforms my work and my life . . . twice, it has drawn me to unimaginable heights.

In *Triumph of Love*, I went on as Princess Leonide two weeks into previews. With all the changes, I probably had two-and-a-half hours on the show. Since this was a musicalized version of a 1732 French comedy, taking place in ancient Sparta, with three disguises (foremost, a young male philosopher), and three seductions (including a woman), Leonide runs a veritable marathon. Even with these stressful circumstances and the limited rehearsal, my work with Sande allowed me to know my lines, my marks, my situations and my objectives. Also who to kiss and when. I opened up my heart to my colleagues and the audience and Leonide came rushing through.

F. Murray Abraham navigated the seven flights of stairs to my dressing room to tell me how wonderful he found working with me.

I like "firsts." I like Sande and the technique. I like performing!

Anitra Frazier

I was working on Broadway for about 15 years before I found The Sande Shurin Acting Studio. I was in the original casts of some of those shows that are being revived now—*How to Succeed...*, *Bye, Bye Birdie* and *Company*. I sang and danced and I had good acting instincts but I kept searching for an acting school that would turn my instincts into a dependable technique I could draw upon at will, instead of waiting for "the magic" to happen.

An example of waiting for the magic happened when I was in *How to Succeed...* Bob Fosse hired me. I had worked for him before in *Redhead* and I felt very honored that he wanted to use me again. Although he had the reputation of being very demanding, a veritable slave driver, his casts invariably adored him because he brought out the best in each of us. I was hired to sing, dance, do three small parts and understudy Rosemary, the ingenue lead.

When the show had run a year they sent out a touring company. I elected to stay in New York and thought no more about it until its stage manager, Phil Friedman, called me from Norfolk, Virginia, on the morning of the day they were supposed to open. The actress playing Rosemary had laryngitis; could I fly down to Norfolk to play the part opening night?

"You're joking," I said. "I've never even met these people, let alone rehearsed with them. Will there be time for a run through?"

"Well, actually, no," he replied and rushed on, "but you'll be alright. The costumes are all the same as the Broadway company; you'll be able to tell who's who by the colors."

I couldn't believe what I was hearing.

"And Sherman is down here for the opening; he'll be right there in the pit."

Sherman Frank, our Broadway conductor, was a veritable rock of Gibraltar. Still, I was not thrilled at the prospect of making a fool of myself in front of a large audience plus the press.

Then Phil played his trump card, "Bob Fosse's here too, you know. He's the one who told me to call you. He says you can do it."

So that was that. How could I disappoint Bobby? I'd just have to jump in and sink or swim.

I arrived two hours before curtain and was informed that the regular Rosemary was feeling a bit better. She would try to do it and I would sit out in the audience ready to leap into action if she caved in. So there I sat in the darkened theater, my makeup case on my lap and watched the show begin. The costumes were the same alright and there was good old Sherman in the orchestra pit, but the girl playing Rosemary was interpreting the part completely different from me. As her voice got weaker and weaker I got more and more nervous. How could I take over with a smooth transition? Our two characterizations were like night and day.

Just then the little door below stage left opened and Phil popped out waving like a windmill and mouthing the words, "You're on!"

Time stopped; my mind stopped; my body followed Phil into a dressing room where a dresser dressed me, a hairdresser coiffed me and I put on my makeup—all in six and a half minutes–while my brain spun into high speed trying to figure out how I was going to play this other actress's version of Rosemary. Then Phil was at the door and leading me to the wings for my entrance. It was only a few steps; it couldn't have taken more than 20 seconds, but in that tiny slice of time, I suddenly knew the answer. In between Rosemary's last exit and this entrance several important things had happened to her. Rosemary had changed. It would be logical that she not behave the same as she did before.

I now ride a second wave of my career with Sande's Transformational Acting Technique.

Mark Kassen

I have been working with Sande for years now and I have found that few things can keep you as clear on what you're doing as her Intention/Action. Things happen very quickly on a television or film set, oftentimes there are last minute rewrites. Almost always, things are shot out of sequence. With this in mind, one must know what the character wants and where he is going.

In the TV movie of the week *The Secret,* I starred as a killer, constantly in danger of being caught. In shooting out of sequence, it can be easy to lose your bearings, especially if the stakes are high and the emotional range of the character covers a wide spectrum. The answer for me was to focus on, and be very clear about, my intention/action for each scene.

As an example, there was a day of shooting in which I was required to do a scene in the morning where my character was defending himself at the police station on a murder charge. In the evening I had to shoot the scene in which I was committing the murder. Two very different, complicated scenes shot out of order. With all the variables going on both for myself and the character (his relationship, his situation, etc.), what connected me to the reality of the scene most directly was his intention/action. In a sense it made everything liberatingly simple for me. In both scenes I chose a very specific intention/action. Having placed my focus on that, the rest found its place. By knowing exactly what the character wanted for each scene, the choices I made became a motor that powered the character, allowing him to go wherever the material demanded.

In short, being simple and precise through intention/action gave me the ability to explore the complexity of each situation.

Anthony Rapp

Since I started working with Sande, I think its safe to say my work on character and my ability to transform into character have exploded and expanded beyond anything I would have previously imagined. It has been my great privilege in the last few years to have the opportunity to take on many diverse lives—a snotty Upper East Side college student in the Broadway and film versions of *Six Degrees of Separation,* a laid-back intellectual in the film *Dazed and Confused,* a desperately needy teenage runaway in the stage production of *Trafficking in Broken Hearts,* and a penitent, articulate convicted murderer in the stage production of *Raised in Captivity,* to name some. Ultimately this culminated in the most challenging, rewarding, deeply satisfying experience I've ever had—becoming Mark Cohen in Jonathan Larson's *Rent* on Broadway and in London.

I was somewhat spoiled in this process, since Mark is very much a stand-in for Jonathan himself. So I was able to observe and absorb qualities in Jonathan that became launching points from which I could dive into Mark. Jonathan Larson (the writer)—and Mark—was extraordinarily passionate about his life and his work, which to him were indivisible. So I focused on bringing that passion to life in Mark, using the Qualities Exercise.

In Sande's Qualities Exercise, it is terribly important to work with three distinct qualities, so they can bounce off each other and create incredible possibilities of tension and resonance within a character. So I also observed a relentless drive and energy that Jonathan embodied, and that I could see within Mark as well—no matter what the circumstances were at the moment, they both pressed on and pressed on. So I had "passionate" and "relentless" to work with. I needed a third, and there was something there, but it was somewhat difficult to articulate. Mark is a filmmaker, and Jonathan was a composer, and both used their lives, and their friends' lives, in their work. So they were observers and recorders. "Passionate" and "relentless" meant getting involved, getting your hands dirty. So "observer and recorder" together were the third quality which is in opposition to "passionate" and "relentless." Even though they were observers and recorders, they were not removed exactly—they were detached but deeply involved. I found this to be the most potent springboard to bring everything together and launch me into the richest experience of transforming into Mark.

Since Jonathan is no longer with us, I felt enormously honored and grateful that I had the opportunity to share with the audience of *Rent* some of what made Jonathan so extraordinary. His incredible passion, his relentless idealism and drive, and his quality of being detached but deeply entwined and caught up in his friends' lives are certainly aspects of what gave him the ability to create *Rent*. In much the same way, they are what gave my character of Mark the ability to create his films.

PART SEVEN

The Spirit Of Acting

The Spirit Of Acting

The following topics speak to that invisible part within us which nourishes and strengthens our inner power.

The spirit of acting deals with the inner world, the humanity and growth of the actor.

Acting comes from the spirit and the spirit is invisible. Artists work with these invisible forces making them visible. We can recognize these forces as dreams, intuitions or new impulses, which help the actor to transform into character, and make the inner connections that are needed to find the moments of the script.

Not all inner connections are about the emotional body or about emotional referencing. An entry point into creating the inner map can be physical, sensorial or just preempted by the preconscious.

This inner map leads you through the material on a personal level, so that it is real to you. Only then will it be meaningful to an audience.

In the foreword, I say that I want to see my actors fly, I want to see them soar into the unknown, raw, bold, risking and with "edge." That is exactly what it takes, wings to fly and wings to soar. Acting is an occupation that breaks through the boundaries of skin and the centers of logic. It takes place in the world of the spirit, beyond time as we know it, into nonlinear time.

Acting lives in spontaneity and intuition. On occasion, it is an intimate communication that is seen by hundreds, thousands, sometimes millions of people. It can be an unfolding of a character's life from birth to death shown in two hours. The actor has to live a life of intense emotions and challenges that would take us years in "real life" time.

We are in the 21st century and very savvy about elements beyond the physical plane. Kirlin photography has documented them, physics accounts for them, best-selling authors such as Deepak Chopra, and Gary Zukav praise them and the actor lives them!

Risk

The inner benefits of risk are as vital as the outer results already spoken of. Risk is a key factor in keeping you energized and on point. Risk triggers a chemical response within your brain that invigorates and makes you wake up ready to go. Taking risks is a potent, positive motivation to your staying on purpose and completing your project.

Taking risks equates with going beyond your limitations, your boundaries, your current frame of reference and your limiting mental chatter. As you challenge yourself to take risks, your perception shifts and you see new possibilities. You dare, and challenge your walls of limitations, and push them out.

Whether leaping across the room, exposing a vulnerable part of yourself, feeling what is unplanned, throwing a chair across the room, or touching someone, it's all risk. It is a risk to use yourself 100 percent and bring those very personal, crazy (I say that affectionately) parts of you foreground. I watch all these fabulous, irrational, unique things we do, yet I don't always see it on stage or on the screen.

BRING IT IN. WHO ARE YOU, THAT YOU ARE NOT BRINGING INTO YOUR WORK YET?

Being risky is working without a formula. And a good technique gets you on track so that you can do just that.

Strong technique but...NO REPEATED FORMULA.

Each script has to be approached in a different way. Yes, some of the things you look at are going to be the same, but what leads you into the script is always different and what it brings up in you changes. Also, you are different with each script. Scripts come to you at different periods in your life, where your circumstances are different and what is relevant changes. Do not imitate yourself, do not become a caricature of who you thought you were in your last performance. Keep yourself creative and open to surprises.

Passion

An actor has to be in touch with his passion. We understand passion sexually, but also need it emotionally and creatively. When we are engaged in sex we are in the moment, having a meaningful experience to focus on. We also know that we have to set inhibitions aside and come from a place of re-sponse. We take action and we respond simultaneously. It's natural; we allow it to occur. That very same mechanism has to be engaged for acting.

Passion is a stronger expression of energy and intensity than we normally experience. We're used to expressing only within a certain degree or range and with a modicum of civility. To ex-press the passion you feel, you have to develop the emotional muscle for it.

Whether you are working in theater or film, your passion has to come from the same inner emotional impulse and heat.

Look at this list of words synonymous with passion and see how passion is indigenous to a performer—actually, any artist. We need to be aware of passion and give ourselves the license to express it.

intense	moving	affecting	eloquent
fervent	dramatic	strong	spirited
inspiring	expressive	excitable	

As I've mentioned before, emotions are made up of two dis-tinct planes. The lower plane emotions include anger, fear, loss and jealousy; the higher plane includes joy, happiness, ecstasy, rapture and bliss. The emotions of the lower plane connect to circumstances in our lives. Most of us don't want to feel the lower plane emotions. We do whatever is necessary to avoid in-tensifying these emotions, even to the point of shutting out de-sire. But we must feel them in order to feel passion. It's a matter of coming into the truth of who we are. We don't want to feel our own hatred, jealousy or greed. Yet these emotions give us very potent energy, even though we judge these emotions as not being good. Look around you, your sister, your brother, your best friend, the people you admire all experience lower plane feelings such as terror and viciousness. It's part of humanity. We have it all and all of us have it. This truth is needed not only to grow but also to make connections into your character. You can't identify only with your character's good qualities. The entire orchestra of the emotional body is what feeds passion.

Allow yourself to be VULNERABLE and let your SELF show (including your embarrassment and your fears). Feeling what you don't want to feel and feeling what you're trying to hide are the key to opening your instrument. What are you vulnerable to? Stand with it; don't run from it. Including the darker side of you, is germane for your growth.

Your growth also depends on your alignment with your soul. You can only see yourself as you already know yourself to be, so you must always have something out in front of you—a possibility or vision that leads you to what's next. Your soul leads you into living something bigger for your life. The soul is why you are here. It carries within it your purpose; and your purpose will give you passion.

Gratitude

When things are great in your life, be sure to give thanks. When things are not so good, find something to be grateful for. I tell actors to make a list of 100 things to be grateful for. It helps you see things in a new perspective. It brings you to a fuller relationship with your soul and your spirit. When you connect with the spirit that you are, you will feel an exhilarating energy. This energy links your self in your physical form and the outer regions of your spirit that connect to the invisible world. This is where the actor and creativity live. Spirit sees possibility that your will often negates before it has a chance to manifest. Your job is to open the doors and let the spirit guide you. Acting begins with the spirit.

This is a time of the HEART—of breaking cycles so your work is done in joy. The heart reconciles the spirit and the will because It is the center of your character. The heart turns all of our mistakes into knowing better for the next time around.

We know that a key to acting is SURRENDER. But the actor often asks, "How do I surrender?" To surrender is to open yourself to a major force, to let things be as they are. Let go of defenses, attitudes and decisions, and surrender to our feelings, instincts and impulses.

Through surrender we are lifted out of . . . We are extricated from . . . We transcend our actual boundaries. When we do this we don't hold ourselves as we actually know ourselves to be . . . We have reached a new octave, playing a new chord—a higher exalted force.

To achieve all of this you must ALLOW it. Allow the energy and the information to work on you. Allow yourself to assimilate it. Allow yourself to transform. Allow yourself to take risks and work with passion.

The invisible forces, the actor's inner essence and spirit, as well as his emotional instrument, all form the rich core that is to become "character." This gives us a place to start from.

This is what distinguishes the "new acting" . . . Transformational Acting: The spirit and soul of the actor is in the game with you, whether for the joy of expressing itself, or the healing, or even to remind us that we are acting to fulfill our purpose.

Afterword

At eight years old my mother would put me on a train in Brooklyn and I would travel to my father's house on Park Avenue and East 37th Street in Manhattan by myself. As we crossed over the bridge I would stand up and look out of the window at the beautiful lights of the city coming toward me. I was truly aware of the distinct difference in energy that came up in me when we crossed into the island of Manhattan. I promised myself that I would someday get out of Brooklyn and live in and be part of the glamour of New York City.

As I conclude this book, we are again in a state of transition, having just become Shurin Levy Enterprises. Bruce and I have constructed a new acting studio in Manhattan's Broadway theater district which houses a 50-seat theater, 48 lights and a computerized lighting board, classrooms, a green room and offices that house three talent agents, a theater company and a lighting designer. I learned early on that anything is possible. There are always new possibilities to be explored, and time after time, although I have stepped into creating what is new for myself and others, I have never done it gracefully and easily. I hit my own walls and stand with my own terror every time I change my life and move into the unknown. I wait until I feel a stir of exhilaration, and then I know that more of me is into the new than the old. That calms my fear. It's the same as rid-ing that train from Brooklyn to New York City. In Brooklyn I was terrified about the ride alone to my father's house. By the time I was halfway across the bridge I was thrilled at the prospect.

You know the rest...for now!

About the Author

SANDE SHURIN, creator of Transformational Acting, teaches her technique at her Times Square acting studio and theatre as well as her Woodstock, New York, center. Ms. Shurin also privately coaches many notable actors in film, theatre, and television, including Anthony Rapp, Matthew Modine, Daphne Rubin-Vega, and rap star Method Man.

Ms. Shurin's theatre company, "Drifting Traffic," was one of five companies to form the Off-Off Broadway Alliance (OOBA). On Broadway she directed the play *The Prince of Genius,* and on cable TV the series *Working Actors.* In her early years, Ms. Shrin premiered three Leonad Melfi plays, *Ah! Wine, Sweet Suite,* and *Beautiful.* She has also directed at the Brooklyn Academy of Music (BAM), the Lincoln Center Festival, and such distinguished Off-Broadway companies as Playwrights Horizons, Theatre for the New City and WPA.

Internationally, Ms. Shurin lectures and leads workshops and intensives. She has also developed the BreakThru Acting workshop, a powerful, transformational event that supports actors in achieving many new and dynamic breakthroughs in their work and their lives.

Ms. Shurin lives and works with her partner and husband, the talent agent and playwright Bruce Levy, in New York City and Woodstock.